THE ULTIMATE SNORKELING BOOK

How to Buy, Upgrade, and Use Snorkeling Equipment,
Identify and Understand Aquatic Animals and their Ecosystems,
Keep Safe, Swim Better, Plan Trips,
Protect Our Living World,
And Have Great Fun

BY

Wes Burgess, M.D., Ph.D.

For Muggsy, my faithful friend.

A Whippet Book

The Ultimate Snorkeling Book
How to Buy, Upgrade, and Use Snorkeling Equipment, Identify and Understand Aquatic Animals and their Ecosystems, Keep Safe, Swim Better, Plan Trips, Protect Our Living World, and have Great Fun.

Copyright © 2010 by Wes Burgess
Cover photograph and figures copyright © 2010 by Wes Burgess
All rights reserved. No part of this book may be reproduced, scanned or distributed in any print or electronic form without permission from the author except in the case of brief quotations or figures embodied in critical articles or reviews.

LIBRARY OF CONGRESS CATALOGING-IN-PUBLICATION DATA

Burgess, Wes
The ultimate snorkeling book / how to buy, upgrade, and use snorkeling equipment, identify and understand aquatic animals and their ecosystems, keep safe, swim better, plan trips, protect our living world, and have great fun / Wes Burgess
    p.   cm.
  Includes bibliographical references (p.   )
  ISBN 978-1-45154443-5
  1. Snorkeling 2. Diving 3. Ocean 4. Fish 5. Sports 5. Nature 6. Ecology 7. Marine Biology
  I. Title

CONTENTS

Introduction...iv

Chapter 1. What Is Snorkeling?.. 1

Chapter 2. Snorkeling Gear: What You Need for the Most Fun...................... 6

Chapter 3. Fine Tuning Your Gear: Why Paying the Most Won't Get You the Best............ 23

Chapter 4. The Right Moves: Great Swimming Strokes for Snorkelers............ 27

Chapter 5. Making the Plunge: What to Do when You Get to the Water......... 33

Chapter 6. The Reef Habitat: What to See and how to See It........................ 42

Chapter 7. Congenial Creatures of the Reef: Fascinating Fish and Interesting Invertebrates 51

Chapter 8. Animals to Watch Out for: Some Are Dangerous and Others Are Just Maligned 62

Chapter 9. Safety First For Adults, Children and Families............................ 72

Chapter 10. Snorkel With Wes: An Everyday Snorkeling Adventure.............. 77

Chapter 11. How to Pack for A Snorkeling Trip... 83

Chapter 12. Snorkeling Seminar: Answers to Your Snorkeling Questions........ 88

Appendix. Resources and Bibliography... 96

Disclaimer... 100

The Author.. 100

Epilog: The Song of the Fireworm.. 100

INTRODUCTION

Unlike SCUBA divers, who have their own worldwide training and accreditation programs, snorkelers have traditionally had to learn about their sport from friends, Internet sites or trial and error, while making plenty of mistakes along the way. Even if you go to a resort, you are likely to be handed a cheap mask and snorkel and left to fend for yourself, without guidance on how to snorkel properly. At this moment, there are no other books devoted to snorkeling, written by a snorkeler, to help you learn to select and use equipment, avoid underwater dangers, understand the aquatic ecosystem, plan trips and prevent costly gaffs that could ruin your snorkeling experience. This book changes all that.

The Ultimate Snorkeling Book is like a personal mentorship with an experienced snorkeler and zoologist. It is as if we were sitting together at my home while I share my hard-won snorkeling information, special techniques, exciting experiences and snorkeling passion.

If you are a beginning snorkeler, *The Ultimate Snorkeling Book* will allay your fears, insure that you are safe and help you experience first-hand the wonders of the teaming life that inhabits our aquatic world. If you are a beginner accompanying an experienced snorkeler, you will find out how to keep up with your partner, share equally in the enjoyment of the sport and add some helpful suggestions of your own during the trip. Even if you do not consider yourself a strong swimmer, you will learn special snorkel swimming techniques that will help you master the reef and have you swimming with the grace of the fish.

If you are an expert already, this book will remind you why you love to snorkel. It will introduce you to some new viewpoints and teach you practical new tips and techniques that you will use as soon as you push off into the water.

The Ultimate Snorkeling Book covers all the important aspects of snorkeling gear, including how each piece of equipment works and what to buy at every price range. There are instructions on how to customize your snorkeling equipment for best performance and how to upgrade your cheap old mask, fins and snorkel so they will perform like professional gear. It will help you build practical maintenance habits to ensure that your equipment is always in top shape throughout your trip.

Through *The Ultimate Snorkeling Book*, you will learn how to protect yourself from burning sun, cold water, leaky masks, tiny jellyfish and big scary fish. If you snorkel as a family, you will learn how you can anticipate children's special needs to keep them safe. You will learn how to prepare for the unexpected so you and your party will come back home healthy and happy.

The Ultimate Snorkeling Book will help you identify the creatures you are seeing and understand why they look and act the way they do. You will understand the fragile shoreline ecosystem and learn how to protect it.

The Ultimate Snorkeling Book will help you plan your trip, get to your destination with everything you need and know exactly what to do when you step into the water. This book also contains removable pre-trip checklists of clothing, equipment, first aid and other essentials. *The Ultimate Snorkeling Book* helps assure that your snorkel trip is a success, no matter what happens.

Whether you travel to resorts in the Bahamas, reef-side bungalows in Fiji or just take a day trip to the nearest inland lake, you can have a great time snorkeling. Once you get started, your equipment, knowledge and skills will last the rest of your life. Let's start right now!

CHAPTER 1
WHAT IS SNORKELING?

Snorkeling is the most exciting and rewarding activity in the world. Snorkeling is an opportunity to enter new worlds, to be overwhelmed by color, pattern and design, and to understand a living, interdependent ecosystem that is a microcosm of our own. In short, snorkeling is a lot of fun.

This book will help you have the most fun possible while you are snorkeling. If you are a beginner, it will introduce you to an exciting sport that may become a lifetime passion. If you are already an old hand at the art of snorkeling, you will learn how to make your experience even more worthwhile. Let's start by clarifying what snorkeling is and what it isn't.

SNORKELING

In this book, when I say snorkeling, I mean a *sport* where people swim on the surface of the water, breathing through a tube and looking through a swim mask or goggles at what is below them. Usually, snorkelers will be wearing flexible swim fins to help propel them through the water. In this book, I am primarily concerned with snorkeling in relative shallow water at the shore or the edge of a reef, where there is plenty of sunlight and oxygen, because that is where the animal life is concentrated.

Skin Diving

The term *skin diving* can be used to refer to any situation where a swimmer is purposely under the water without a heavy suit or diving bell. Snorkeling is a form of skin diving.

Free Diving

When people speak of *free diving*, they usually are referring to energetic individuals wearing masks and fins who gasp a great lungful of air and try to dive deeply while holding their breath. Snorkelers, on the other hand, spend most or all of their time cruising on the surface, breathing through their snorkels. By the way, if you are breathing through your snorkel and choose to dive deep, your snorkel will probably fill up with water and you are likely to get a mouthful.

SCUBA Diving

The term SCUBA was coined by co-inventor Jacques Cousteau as an acronym for **S**elf-**C**ontained **U**nderwater **B**reathing **A**pparatus. Although there are many kinds of diving, when I say *diving*, I will be referring to SCUBA diving.

I have great respect for SCUBA diving as a sport and as a social culture unto itself. Only SCUBA will allow you to face the depths of the waters. However, a SCUBA diver loaded up with heavy tanks, a lead weight-belt and a thick rubber suit trailing noisy bubbles, is a far cry from the lithe, green profile of the snorkeler skimming quietly and gently across the surface of the water, intimately sharing the fragile, shallow aquatic habitat with its natural inhabitants. Snorkeling has its own special beauty, offers great physical exercise and provides a window into the most secret of aquatic worlds. Snorkeling is its own sport with its own body of dedicated adherents. That is why it deserves this book.

Why Snorkel?

Snorkeling is God's own sport and it is the closest thing to heaven I have ever found. Picture yourself lying in warm, sunny water, watching a 5-star movie unfold in front of your eyes—snorkeling is like that, but even better. If I can help you get even a small portion of the enjoyment I get out of snorkeling, then you will have something to treasure for the rest of your life.

Most of our modern culture is about bigness—the biggest houses, the biggest salaries, the biggest babies and so forth. Most sports are about bigness, also—the big game, the big team, the big star, the big pitch, shot, pass or drive. By comparison, snorkeling is little, little, little. You will find the brightest colors on the tiniest little crabs no bigger than a nickel. The smallest fish swim in groups afire with neon reds, yellows and blues. The most fascinating ecosystems on the planet are just a few feet below the surface.

Imagine you are suspended calmly, a few feet from the most beautiful and exciting animals that you could possibly imagine. More diverse and colorful than any zoo, the reefs provide you with a close-up look at their diverse inhabitants living in their natural habitat, going about their daily lives for you to experience and share. In a single morning of snorkeling, thousands of brilliantly colored ocean creatures pass before you in a vibrant microcosmos, performing the same behaviors that they have done for thousands of years for your entertainment and edification. You could snorkel in the same place every day for a year and still see new things every day. In contrast, if you were SCUBA diving, you would be 30-100 feet down in the deep, cold waters, with hundreds of pounds strapped to your back, peering through the dim light and lurking seaweed in hopes of seeing something to tell your friends about over dinner. After they tell their story, you will recall the myriad of wonders you have seen snorkeling and smile. To borrow from the great philosopher Lao Tse, it is because snorkeling is little that it becomes big.

Snorkeling provides an opportunity for an organic break with the artificial constraints of our big-oriented daily world. It is a green experience. Every time you leave the water after snorkeling, you will be more impressed with the need to preserve our natural world.

Where Should I Snorkel?

You can snorkel anywhere the water is warm, clear, shallow, and filled with life. Some great snorkeling places are well known, some take a little effort to find and some are secret places that you will discover and keep for yourself. These secret spots will become the legacy of a lifetime of snorkeling.

As soon as you have the right stuff, you will be able to snorkel everywhere, and I encourage you to do so. This book mostly covers snorkeling on and around tropical reefs and shores, because these are the places where I enjoy snorkeling most. These shallow waters on top of coral and sand contain animal life at its most abundant, diverse and beautiful. I especially enjoy snorkeling in the Caribbean—the Antilles, Jamaica, the Bahamas, Puerto Rico and all points in between. I also snorkel off the coast in Florida and California where the animal life is not always so diverse but is often much more accessible.

I also enjoy snorkeling inland in fresh water. There are wonderful opportunities for snorkelers in any of the United States' recreational lakes. I have spent plenty of time snorkeling in dug-out ponds on farms and private property. If you plan to snorkel a lot in fresh water, be sure to see the section on coastal and freshwater snorkeling in Chapter 5.

NEWBIES

I always feel compassionate when I see a pair of swimmers paddling around far, far from the shore wearing yellow plastic children's snorkeling gear and staring down into 100 feet of empty water. What are they looking at? Nothing, because all the life is in the warm, oxygenated, sunny, shallow water 6-20 feet from the shore or reef. If only someone had led them into the shallow water, they would have been amazed, but because they do not know where to look, they are doomed to spend their day chugging across the ocean peering down into the cold, deep sterile water, watching the coral, seaweed and sponges weave to and fro, far away on the dark ocean floor.

These poor fish will probably come back to the bar in the evening and tell their companions, "I tried snorkeling today. It's terrible! You can't see anything and you are bashed around by the waves. I'm going to spend the rest of my vacation sitting around the pool."

I was curious to know what these tyros were seeing, so one day I swam out away from the shore. On the way, I looked down and saw lots of white sand kept company by an occasional blue wrasse, or a lonely yellow goatfish. The fish were pretty pale, as if they were feeling self-conscious for being out so far from their colorful schoolmates cavorting in the warmth and oxygen. As the water deepened, I saw massive clumps of seaweed and corals but even these giants looked pretty small from the surface and the water was so dark at that distance that they looked more like shadows than animals. Finally, I saw a beautiful green sea turtle. Although he was hard to make out, he was glorious. I estimate my turtle was about 3 feet in diameter but at the distance I saw him, he looked about one-quarter-inch long.

After seeing my tiny turtle, I swam back to the warm, calm, shallow reefs. There I could count on seeing at least 25 or more bejeweled fish at any time, many of them as big as my head.

FIVE BASIC SNORKELING CONCEPTS

To snorkel, you need a minimum of equipment—a mask, fins and a snorkel—and a place to get into the water. With these few tools, you will glide along the surface of the shallow water, watching the teaming life below. Your enjoyment will be enhanced with practice and the understanding of some basic snorkeling principles that help you see more and keep safe. Here are some basic suggestions that will help you get the most out of your snorkeling.

1. Don't Hurry! Have Your Fun in the Sun

Water moves in its own time, so try to sense this and synchronize with it. Snorkeling isn't a race. There's no prize for swimming the farthest or seeing the most in the least time. The most important thing about snorkeling is having fun.

There is an unlimited spectrum of things to see if you are willing to take your time. A Los Angeles photographer specializing in fish photos put this into perspective. He said, "My camera equipment is top-notch. I have everything I need to handle any situation. My problem is that I can't find anything new to photograph." His problem was that he was moving too fast. I have never run out of exciting things to see when snorkeling, as long as I have taken my time. If I get bored, I just slow down and observe more carefully and I begin to see things I missed before.

I did an experiment that helped clarify this concept. On one snorkeling trip, instead of trying to visit as many island sites as possible, I decided to spend the whole trip snorkeling the same small rocky outcrop every afternoon. The more times I hung over that outcrop, the more I saw. In fact, I calculated that I had seen more new species of marine life by revisiting the same site than I had previously seen while visiting different sites that were far apart.

For example, the first day I saw a new species of feather duster, a 1-2-inch reef-dwelling animal that extends a crown of feathery appendages to collect food from the ocean. I saw this specimen under a rock crevice, and although I searched and searched, I could find no more. The second day I found the same feather duster in the same crevice but I found five more that had been in plain view all the time. By the end of the week, I was seeing these new feather dusters all over the rocky outcrop. They had all been in plain sight before but I had not observed them. With continued observation, I began to understand their pattern of distribution and their favorite habitat types, as well as to learn how they obtained food and avoided predators. I began to understand their role in this coral ecosystem. If I had just grabbed a hasty glance and hurried on, I would have missed everything.

Another experiment also showed me the wisdom of slowing down. One day, just for fun, I decided to spend the whole day parked in the water above two tiny nimble spray crabs hanging out in and around the black spines of small sea urchins (see Chapters 7 and 8). As I began to observe them, I found that there were really six crabs of different sizes living under cover of the urchins. I was able to see the neon yellow color on the joints of their spindly black legs and the tiny arms that they used to pass food into their little mouths. I saw how they chose when and where to hide when a shadow went by and how the six of them interacted when they came close to each other or dove for the same hiding place. I saw tiny schools of baby fish taking refuge in the spines of the urchin and watched them move in unison as bigger fish approached or as the waves pushed them to and fro. I am sure that if I had spent a week just watching the crabs around those sea urchins I would have continued to see more and learn more every day.

2. Stay Quiet

If you thrash around in the water, the fish will be perturbed, and you will look like a jackass. The best posture for observing shallow marine life is laying dead in the water, floating on your stomach, body relaxed and head looking down. I think that fish are disturbed by fish-sized moving hands, so you should keep your arms close to your body, unless you need them for swimming. With practice, you will learn to move in and out with the waves, arms tight to your body, controlling your position with the slightest of movements and completely camouflaged from the creatures underneath.

As you learn to snorkel quietly, you will be able to observe the intricate workings of the underwater ecosystem. You will get to know the creatures of the reef, how they live their lives, why they do what they do, and how everything you see fits into the ecosystem of the reef.

I was once asked for help by a snorkeler who said, "Wes, I go to the same places you do, I take my time, and I look like crazy, but I don't see nearly as much. What am I doing wrong?"

I offered to snorkel with him that morning and I quickly found the source of his trouble. He flailed his arms and legs so artlessly that he churned clouds of bubbles in the water all around him. Against the sun, he was constantly projecting rapidly moving shadows that sent the reef creatures running for cover. In shallower water, he created sand storms on the bottom with his fins. When I closed my eyes and listened, all I could hear was his noisy thrashing in the water. Moreover, unbeknownst to him, he had a habit of humming noisily as he breathed through his snorkel. When I explained what was happening and he quieted down, he was satisfied with all he could then see—and hear—under the water.

3. Never Snorkel in Water that Is over Your Head

Although you will find good spots that are deeper, shallow water is the best place to snorkel. Marine life requires a combination of light, oxygen and warmth to proliferate. If you want to observe a shoreline ecosystem, stay where the action is. Besides, most of the interesting sights will be small creatures and you have to be close enough to see them if you want to learn their secrets. Stick to the shallow water. Now if you find a lagoon or reef where the water is 7-feet deep, you can still snorkel there, but shallower water is better if it is available.

Shallow snorkeling is also safe snorkeling. While researching *The Ultimate Snorkeling Book*, I made a list of all the dangers that divers and other snorkelers warned me about, including cramps, driving winds, fatigue, hypothermia, powerful waves, storms and tide changes. It dawned on me that almost everything they considered dangerous would pose a minimal threat if you were snorkeling in shallow water.

By the way, with a little practice you can snorkel comfortably in surprisingly shallow water. In Lac Bay on the island of Bonaire, I snorkeled for hours in just two feet of water, watching the plant and animal life on the sandy bottom habitat.

4. Do Not Disturb

If I can convince you of only one thing, this is it: do not touch anything in the water anywhere at any time. Shallow marine ecosystems are fragile and each species depends on finding and creating its ideal microhabitat. The lives and behavior of all the species in each reef ecosystem are in delicate balance. Whenever you pick up or disturb an organism or its habitat, you are upsetting the gentle balance that is responsible for the very ecosystem you have come to see. In shorter words—you are screwing things up for everybody.

I don't like to see gloves and I advise against wearing them or associating with those who do. Gloves mean that a person is prepared to touch things. Ocean creatures sting, bite and scrape painfully for a reason. They don't want to be touched.

After all, you are visiting the natural homes of these aquatic creatures. You should show some respect for other living things. For example, just touching coral makes it die. You may say, "Yeah, there's lots of coral. Who cares?" But between anchors, coral harvesting, storms and tourists, world coral populations are on the decline. Because coral is the backbone of the reef habitat, decreased coral populations threaten the health of reef habitats worldwide. Besides, we are supposed to be the sentient beings on this planet. Why then do we need to kill animals left and right just because we are passing through their natural habitat area?

I've noticed an increasingly touchy tendency in guides and instructors lately. Some snorkeling and diving teachers feel they have to grab and manhandle the local fauna to impress their students with a hands-on demonstration. However, as soon as you pull a shrimp, fish or coral colony to the surface and handle it, you have lost all opportunity to see the creature in its natural habitat and have probably killed the creature as well. I remember when a marine biologist disappeared under the water, only to reappear and place a poor foot-long cylindrical creature in my hands. "Here, it's a sea cucumber," she said. "Take a look."

If this ever happens to you, you have a choice of what to do. You could say, "Thanks. I realize you are well-meaning, but I am here to see marine life in its natural environment and I cannot do that if the habitat is disturbed." Or, you could just say, "What are you doing, you goober? Put that thing back right now!"

Another example of *noli me tangere* applies to eels (see Chapter 8). Now I like eels. They have pretty colors; they're interesting creatures with a cryptic, mostly nocturnal behavioral strategy; and they have an exciting life history with a simplified larval form, group migration, metamorphoses and complex solitary adult specialization. When you find a beautifully spotted moray eel in her hole, keep your fingers out. Eels can bite if you stick your fingers too close to their mouths but you will never be in risk if you don't go out of your way to touch them.

5. Don't Snorkel Alone

Now it's time for a confession. I sometimes end up snorkeling alone because I want to snorkel all the time, whereas my friends and family get tired and seem to want to waste their time eating, sleeping and pursuing other nonsnorkeling activities. However, I believe that the buddy system is always preferable for safety's sake.

I remember snorkeling by myself off the reefs near La Parguera, Puerto Rico. These reefs are a ways off shore and I had a friend drop me off in his boat. When he left, there was no one around to help me if I got into trouble.

The water was warm and clear. As often happens near reefs, I bumped into some coral underwater and I was bleeding from a calling card-sized scrape on my leg. Suddenly, I noticed the blood in the water and I became scared. I started looking around for sharks, barracuda and other unknown but potentially dangerous creatures. What if I was bitten, suffered a cramp, or ran into the stinging arms of a giant jellyfish? These waters were unknown to me. What if currents or winds came and drove me far out into the ocean? I started treading water furiously, looking for my friend, although I knew that he was not due back for two hours. Suddenly I had a great awareness of the vastness of the ocean and the fragile limits of my own mortality.

I quickly calmed down and swam slowly back to a coral head where I climbed out and waited until my leg stopped bleeding. By the time my friend picked me up, I had a chance to think about how quickly and easily a perilous situation can develop if you are snorkeling alone. What if I *had* been in serious danger? I've never been bothered by big fish while swimming with a partner. If I had an accident, an injury or even just a cramp, I could have counted on my buddy to get me out of the water and to medical help if needed.

I am telling you this because I don't want you to be scared like I was. Just snorkel with a partner and everything will be fine.

WHAT'S TO COME?

In the ensuing pages, I hope to challenge your mind, open your eyes to new sights and help you exercise your body safely in an active sport. I'll tell you all about how to get started, how to improve your snorkeling and how to eliminate problems before they start. You'll get the benefit of my mistakes and my skills that have taken years to acquire. I hope to tell you things you will not hear anywhere else.

I don't offer this information lightly. You may just be hooked on this low-impact, high-excitement sport. You may even experience changes in your sense of yourself when you begin to observe reef creatures and understand their lives. Like me, you could find that snorkeling becomes a life passion, transforming your own world.

The ancient waters can become your sanctuary, your entertainment and your teacher. But it does not happen automatically. You will need a minimum of equipment, a good place to snorkel and an understanding of what to do once you are in the water.

CHAPTER 2

SNORKELING GEAR:

WHAT YOU NEED FOR THE MOST FUN

In the beginning, life was simple. I had a blue rubber Voit mask with a round glass lens—designed for use in a suburban swimming pool—and a pair of rubber Voit slip-on fins. They weren't just the best fins in my little hometown store; they were the only fins. I got my snorkel from the Green Stamps store. It had a 180-degree bend at both ends and looked like a long, skinny C. It had a backwash valve that consisted of a little rubber ball in a cage. When you submerged too deep, the little ball closed against the end of the snorkel, keeping water—and air—out of the tube.

Well, I quickly sawed off the valve because it was so lame, leaving me with a straight tube pointing out of the water, and believe it or not, this hodge-podge gear worked well for many years of snorkeling. Here's the motto of this story: if you plan to spend more than $20 on snorkeling equipment, then it had better work better than my first outfit or you're being ripped off shamelessly.

YOUR MASK

The purpose of your mask is to allow you to see in the water. That's it! There are many manufacturers out there with many models to choose from (see the Appendix), but if you find a mask that you can see through and doesn't leak, you are in business. The rest is just icing on the cake.

The recent history of diving masks is simple. Masks started out as a wide rubber tube with your face at one end and a round slab of window glass about 8 inches away. These masks gave you tunnel vision and encouraged condensation. They either fell off in the water or made your face look puckered up as if it had been stuck up a drainpipe all day because you had to torque the strap so tight to your head to keep the mask from leaking. After a couple of years, the natural rubber began to crumble into dust. Nevertheless, without any technological advantages at all, these masks from the Cretaceous period of snorkeling worked OK and allowed the snorkeler to have a lot of fun.

Innovations have come in four aspects of the mask: 1) the fit, 2) the field of the view, 3) the volume and 4) special features. One or two special features are really cool while the rest are stupid gimmicks that increase your cost and decrease your mask's reliability. Let's start with the fit.

The Fit

The technology that contributes to a well-fitting mask is simply a bead of silicone that runs around your face, enclosing your eyes and nose. The main differences between brands and styles of masks are the dimensions of this gasket. You are likely to hear the same advice everywhere for finding a good-fitting mask: Try on all the masks on in your local store. When you find one that fits, buy it!"

Unfortunately, this advice is not very good. For one thing, some of us do not have a local store. Furthermore, once you get to the store, you will soon realize that they do not have enough of a selection for you to try on. For example, assume each mask manufacturing company makes five different masks, with the same general fit and design. I can easily count 10 major mask manufacturing companies, giving you 50 masks on the market for you to try.

Now you might be lucky to find a store with 25 masks on the wall for you to try. However, most stores only carry masks from one or two different manufacturers, which means that you will only be able to try two styles of fit and design. The rest of the stock is filled up with similarly designed and constructed masks from the same manufacturers that have not sold in previous years. Even if these masks are labeled with different makes and models, you will see that they are more alike than different. And you will also find that they won't have all the sizes available for the styles that they do carry. Consequently, the number of different mask designs you can actually try in one store is not representative of the diversity of masks available for you to buy.

Now, you can just go to other stores if they are within driving range, but by the time you have run all over the place in an attempt to try on all these masks, you will be worn out, out of money from the driving expense and you will probably have a disgusting case of pinkeye from the eye goop and face grease left behind by all the other people who have been trying on the same masks before you. Also, shop clerks are often unhelpful. They will often direct you to the most expensive mask in the shop, regardless of your individual needs.

Furthermore, how do you tell from trying on a mask in the store how it will fit in the water? Everyone will tell you to try out masks by holding them to your face, sucking in your breath and watching to see if they fall off. But you don't go around snorkeling red-faced with your breath sucked in. When you use the mask, you will be in the water, breathing normally, with straps holding the mask lightly to your face, not standing in a store sucking in your breath. I cannot tell for sure whether I will like a mask unless I have worn it for several hours. It sometimes takes a few days of real snorkeling to find out whether a mask is right for you.

Lots of you will be buying masks over the Internet. Web shoppers have access to a broader selection of masks, but there's no way to try them on through an Internet connection. Everyone tells me they will find a mask on the Internet and try it on in the dive shop, but in practice, it is difficult to find a store that carries a mask with the same manufacturer, model and model year as the one you saw on your computer. Also, there is some ethical issue in using the facilities and resources of a store when you know you will be buying your mask somewhere else.

Remember, the biggest cost in buying a mask is having to buy another if you find that you do not like the first one you purchased. Here are my suggestions to make your mask selection as easy as possible. First, look at reviews or specifications and pick a mask that has the widest field of view and the lowest volume, as discussed below. Then find a store or online seller who carries the mask and will allow you to return it for a full refund if you don't like it. Before you buy anything, make sure you understand all about the store or website return policy. Then buy or order your mask. When you get it home, take your mask to the nearest pool, spa or bathtub and try it out. Experiment to find the lightest strap pressure that will hold your mask in place without leaking. Hopefully you'll be amazed at how clearly you can see everything and you'll congratulate yourself on what a pile of money you saved.

I bought my first Ocean View mask like this. I did some homework, decided that Ocean View masks had a broad field of view with low volume, and I ordered the mask directly from the Ocean View website. When the mask arrived, I put it on and immediately jumped into the spa. The mask fit great and stayed on my face with a minimum of strap pressure. There were no leaks and no funny rough places inside the mask to collect condensation. The mask did not drag when I turned my head around and the visibility was great.

Then I gave the mask the long-term test. I just wore it around all day on my head and it remained comfortable after many hours. I did not find any hidden edges to dig holes in my head, and when I finally took the mask off, my face did not look like it had been sucked by the bell of a giant trombone. Perfect. I am now on my second mask from that manufacturer.

If your first mask does not fit as well as you would like, pick a mask with a wide field of view and low volume from another manufacturer. Usually, the fit is similar between different styles within each manufacturer's line. If masks from one manufacturer seem to fit you better, select one of their products when you are looking for your next mask.

Although it isn't widely publicized, masks come in two sizes—regular and small. Sometimes the smaller masks are called youth or junior. No matter what they are called, if you are a woman or man with a small face, concentrate on these masks. Don't even look at the larger sized masks because they won't fit as well.

Your Field of View

Avoid giving yourself the marine version of tunnel vision by selecting a mask with a wide field of view. You want to be able to see as far up, down, left and right as possible. To help understand the importance of field of view, imagine that you are floating gently in warm, sunny water. You can see far enough in every direction that you do not even have to turn your head to see everything of interest in the water. The floor of the ocean is stretched out like a bright white carpet beneath you. Life is good.

However, next to you is a poor fellow who bought a mask with a narrow field of view. With his drainpipe visual field, he must scan the ocean floor like a madman, a few inches at a time. When he tries to follow a fish swimming past, he has to struggle to keep it in sight, as if he were using a cheap pair of binoculars on land. What a terrible fate. Just get a mask with the widest field of vision and you will avoid his misery.

One place to start with this quest is on the Internet, looking at published field of view numbers for a variety of masks. They will usually be given in degrees of vision vertically and horizontally. Even armed with these figures, when you begin trying on masks, you will find the statistics do not generalize well to practical use. Fortunately, I have a portable failsafe technique for you to use to measure your mask's field of view that you can employ in the store or at home.

Start by finding a tiled floor. Otherwise, you will have to get your partner to run around like an idiot with a piece of chalk. Put on the mask in question, bend over with the mask lens parallel to the floor and look down at your feet. That is the center point of your visual field. Now, without moving your head, turn your eyes all the way to the left. Count the number of tiles you see or have your companion mark the farthest point you can see on the floor with chalk and measure it. Now repeat this procedure while looking to the right. This is the width of your horizontal field of view. Do not be surprised if the horizontal field of view of two masks differs as much as 4-6 feet.

Now test your field of view in the vertical direction. Bend over and look at your feet again with the mask lens parallel with the floor. Without moving your head or the mask, look up (forward) with your eyes and measure how many tiles you can see. Unless you have eyes in the back of your head, there is no backwards view, so just double this measurement for the vertical field of view. Only now do you have the information you will need to compare different masks' field of view.

Multiply the left-right number and the up-and-down number to give you a single factor to compare different masks. Based on your research and measurements, take the mask that has the biggest field of view. Remember that intuition and feel play important roles here so be guided by your measurements but not ruled by them.

Mask Volume

The best masks for snorkeling trap only a small amount of air between the mask and your face. These are called low-volume masks. They provide a wider field of view, because with the lenses close to your face your vision is not obstructed by the silicone sides of the mask. They also minimize condensation by reducing the area of silicone on which water vapor can condense. Low-volume masks also offer the least drag resistance when moving through the water, making it easier to swim and turn your head without splashing around. Low-volume masks are less likely to be ripped off your face if you are hammered by a wave in choppy or stormy water or if you dive into the water wearing your mask, although I do not recommend the latter.

If you have a mask on hand, you can calculate its volume exactly. Fill the mask with water and with your head down, put on the mask until the excess water has been displaced. Then carefully take off the mask and pour its contents into a kitchen measuring cup. This will give you an exact measure of the volume of air in a mask while it is on your own, uniquely shaped face. If you are testing two masks, repeat these steps for the other mask and compare.

Or, go to the Internet and search for the published volumes of the masks in which you are interested. You can often find the volume of each mask listed in the manufacturers' product information or on commercial websites. Of course, every company lists volume differently, usually in different units, just to make your life more interesting.

I found the mask volume information for two commercial masks on the Internet and ordered them both sight unseen. Both masks were low volume, but the first provided a generous view from side-to-side whereas the second mask allowed me to see more in front of me. I eventually bought both masks and I have since used them extensively. After much experience, I decided that I liked the side-to-side visibility more than the ability to see farther in the vertical direction. Ultimately, it was the color of the silicone skirt that determined my favorite (see below).

Lenses

Glass or Plastic Lenses?

It used to be that all good lenses were made of high quality glass and plastic lenses were just for kids swimming in the pool. However, polycarbonate changed all that and you should never consider a snorkeling mask with glass lenses. Polycarbonate has more desirable optical properties than glass—my reading glasses are all polycarbonate—because it is lighter and has excellent light-conducting qualities. Also, there is no reason to go around with a material that can break into sharp shards so close to your eyes. Polycarbonate lenses can be made virtually unbreakable so you will not be vulnerable to that bully on the beach.

Tinted versus Color-Corrected Lenses

Tinting is a controversial feature in masks. The first tinted lenses consisted of cheap plastic lenses dyed international yellow. These masks distorted natural colors and made you feel like you were living in Yellowville. You can still find inexpensive masks with amber, blue, gray and rose-colored lenses. Stay away from these monstrosities. They cripple your ability to recognize reef creatures and their cheap plastic lenses scratch and distort your vision.

Color-corrected lenses superficially resemble tinted lenses but they are really quite clever and sophisticated. Color-corrected lenses work like the special color correction filters used in expensive cameras to restore natural colors. For example, color photographs made under fluorescent lights take on a sickly green hue, as if a layer of green shellac had been painted over the print. To avoid this problem, professional photographers buy special color-correcting filters for this and other difficult lighting conditions. When the color-correction filter is placed over the camera lens, the resulting photographs come out in perfect, natural colors.

The ocean also imparts a color of its own, usually a bluish tint, that overlays the natural colors of marine life. The blue color gets darker when you are looking through more water. Knowing this, ophthalmologists have devised special color correction lenses for snorkeling masks. These take away the bluish tint imparted by ocean water so that the natural colors of fish, rocks, coral and so forth are revealed. With the removal of this blue haze, details are clearer and overall vision appears somewhat sharper. I own masks with color-corrected lenses and I think that the increased accuracy and vibrancy of the colors is astounding.

As you have probably guessed by now, the development and application of these color-correction techniques is complicated and relatively expensive. If you are on a budget, you should try masks with color-corrected lenses in the water, first, to see if the effect is worth the extra cost.

Masks with One, Two, Four or More Windows

My first snorkeling masks had a single great *Cyclops*-like lens. Later masks had a separate window for each eye—these are currently in vogue. Assuming that fit, field of view and volume are the same, I find that both designs work equally well and you can take your pick.

You will see many three-lens masks consisting of a narrow central lens with extra windows on the sides. These masks don't provide an uninterrupted view because the side windows are framed by opaque or translucent plastic supports. When you wear these masks, you have to keep turning your head or fish will keep getting lost behind these frames. The center lens in three-window masks almost always provides a narrower view than a traditional single or double lens model. Furthermore, the side windows are usually molded in hard, clear plastic and are not lens quality. Whatever you see through them is distorted and out of focus.

Invariably adding extra windows to the real estate increases the volume of the mask, extending the lenses so far from your face like that it feels like you are looking through binoculars. This extra volume narrows your field of view and increases inside condensation. These monsters add unnecessary drag in the water, causing wave motion to tug them back and forth on your face.

I've tried masks that sport four, five and six separate lenses. How many separate lenses do you need? After all, you only have two eyes. If you were a big cockroach with hundreds of cells arranged into a giant compound eye, it might be different. But you're not—I hope.

My advice is to forget about masks that have more than two windows.

Prescription Lenses

Hey! You, with the owl-eyes who wears glasses for reading, driving and/or distance! If you have trouble seeing objects clearly at distances of 3-10 feet, consider getting corrective lenses in your mask. After all, you might as well chuck this whole book into a Billy goat's mouth if you cannot see what's in the water when you are snorkeling, and if you have not found out already, you won't be able to wear your specs under a diver's mask. If you need distance correction to see well, then you will benefit from special lenses in your mask. Period.

Now, it used to be that only millionaires could afford to have their facemasks ground to their eyeglass prescription, but those days are past. Nowadays you just send your doctor's lens prescription to a major mask maker online and they send you back your customized mask. Turnaround time is usually 10-14 days.

My experience was like this:

- ☑ I visited my eye doctor and received a special prescription for ideal vision at a range between 1-10 feet (30 minutes)
- ☑ I ordered a custom mask online from my favorite mask company, typed in my prescription, and paid with a credit card (15 minutes)
- ☑ My mask arrived at my home in perfect condition (2 weeks)

The total outlay for this mask was 45 minutes of my time, 14 days waiting for the mask to arrive, and about $75-100 extra cost for the custom lenses.

If this still sounds like too much bother, major companies like Body Glove offer correction lenses in weak, medium, and strong strengths for nearsighted vision that are comparable in price to similar brands. You can try these masks on in your local dive shop. Note that correcting lenses may also give your mask a wider field of view.

People always ask me whether they can wear their contact lenses under their masks. There are so many variables involved that I have to yield to the professionals in this matter. Ask your ophthalmologist.

Silicone Skirts: Clear, Black or Day Glo?

The skirt is what wise guys like me call the body of the mask that holds the lens(es) on your face. These silicone tubes may be opaque, translucent or nearly transparent and you can find them in clear, black, international orange, blueberry, raspberry, puce, avocado, and every other color you can imagine. Really, the only reasonable choices are black and nearly clear. I cannot imagine what advantages brightly colored skirts are supposed to confer except to give everyone else a good laugh.

I have heard that clear skirts are better because they increase the light so your pupils constrict and your eyes maintain better focus. I have also heard that opaque black skirts are better because they reduce the light so your pupils dilate and your eyes become more sensitive to light. You cannot have it both ways.

About 5 years ago, I bought two masks that fit well, provided a good field of view and were low volume. The first came only with a clear, almost transparent silicone skirt and the other was only available with an opaque black skirt. After years of trials, I decided that I like the opaque black skirt better. The light and the fuzzy forms visible through the clear silicone skirt were slightly distracting, and at the right angle, sun shining through the water sometimes hurt my eyes. None of these things happened with the black skirt. Nowadays, if a mask I want is available in a black skirt, I'll order that option. However, it is a small difference and it should not rank high on your decision-making tree.

Mustaches and Skirts

No matter what you hear, if you have a mustache and you want to wear a snorkeling mask, you are screwed. I have researched every known solution to keep masks from leaking around my mustache and invented some more on my own and none of them has worked for spit. I tried clipping my mustache quite short, but water still leaked through. I tried shaving the top of my mustache, leaving the lip area directly under my nose naked for the mask to grab, but it did not work and I looked like an idiot for weeks. Maybe if I had a lip as long as an orangutan this might have worked but my ancestors were not that simian. I tried smearing my mustache with Vaseline, KY Jelly, Bardol, Wesson Oil, Astro Lube and clarinet grease. All I made was a mess. Finally, I just shaved the thing off. Everyone tells me I look more stylish, younger and generally more debonair, but the only reason I shaved my mustache off was to get my mask to fit right. If you are a hairy he-man and you can grow your mustache back quickly, then you might just shave your face before every trip. I'll stay smooth, thank you.

By the way, SCUBA divers do not have such a problem with mustaches and leaking masks because the air in their masks is under positive pressure and it tends to drive the water out.

Purge Valves

Some masks also sport valves projecting from the center of the mask. If water gets into your mask, you are supposed to squeeze the purge valve in front of your nose, blow out and force the extra droplets back into the ocean again. Unfortunately, purge valves get in the way of your vision and add volume to the mask, decreasing your field of view and increasing the likelihood of condensation. Purge valves also make the mask project farther into the water, creating more drag when swimming and making it more likely that your mask can be dislodged if you hit a big wave. And you are supposed to pay a premium for all of this nonsense? Phooey.

Fortunately, snorkelers don't need purge valves. If your mask fills up with water, just pop your head out and lift your mask slightly away from your upper lip so the captive water drains out. Then go back to your snorkeling. If your mask lets in lots of water, make a mental note to look for a better-fitting mask when you have finished snorkeling for the day.

MASK DEFOG STRATEGIES

Many people are never troubled with a foggy mask. However, I have always had terrible problems with fog appearing on the inside of my mask. I think the condition hounds me because my face is warm. In some waters, I needed to stop and clear my mask with water every few minutes while snorkeling. After a thorough investigation of the issue, I have much to tell you about preparing your mask to avoid condensation.

So how does a mask fog up, anyway? Well, it clearly is *not* fog that causes the problem. I've walked around on many a foggy day near the ocean but I have never seen any fog appearing *inside* a snorkeling mask. No, so-called fog is really water condensing on the inside of the lens that makes it hard to see through your mask. Water condensing on the inside of the silicone skirt further adds to the problem.

If you remember your chemistry, water exists in three forms: liquid water, invisible water vapor and solid ice. Unless you will be snorkeling in the arctic, we can dispense with the latter. When you put on your mask, you are trapping warm air from the outside environment inside the space between the lens and your face. If you are anywhere near an ocean or a large body of water, it is likely that the conditions will be humid and a lot of invisible water vapor will be included with the air. Furthermore, your skin is constantly giving off water vapor, which will be added to the rest of the water vapor trapped inside your mask. If the surrounding water is cooler than the air around your face, the water vapor will tend to change state and turn back to liquid water. This water congregates around attractive surfaces and condenses there to form droplets, rivulets and pools of liquid water inside the mask. Of course, if you wanted to look through water, you would not have put on a mask in the first place. Since you cannot stick a tiny dehumidifier inside your mask, the next best thing is to prepare the surfaces inside your mask so they will no longer attract water vapor condensation.

Don't Scrub Your Mask with Sand

The first step is cleaning your mask. If your mask is completely cleaned of dust and oils, there will be fewer places for water vapor to condense. Hundreds of years ago, wet sand was rubbed on materials like marble and metal to scrub off tough deposits of dirt and oxidation. These evolved into fancier, more expensive products like Soft-Scrub, Comet, Bon-Ami and cleansers that just contain finer sand. Please, do not use these abrasive substances to clean your mask. Ever.

When I bought my first mask, everyone had the same advice for me. "Scrub it with Crest," they all said. Before I even got my mask home, three sales clerks, the cashier, an elderly couple shopping in the store and some bum in the street all volunteered their advice. "Clean it with Crest," they all said. Even the booklet that came with my mask began by saying, "Clean the mask thoroughly with a popular dentifrice." And what do you think that "popular dentifrice" might be? That's right. *Crest!*

Well, I'm telling you now, *don't* scrub your mask with Crest. The "gentle abrasive" in most toothpastes is silicon particles—another name for sand. Toothpaste is abrasive; it can scratch lenses, damage lens coatings, and produce millions of tiny irregularities that gather water and cause your mask to fog. Just think about it. Does your mask look like a tooth? Does it look like a bullet-shaped object with a porcelain surface so hard that it scratches metal? Or does it look like a poor, delicate, vulnerable little piece of plastic in a silicone sandwich? Don't scrub your mask with Crest!

That said, I've tried everything other than Crest to clean my mask and reduce its propensity to fog. I've tried liquid dishwashing detergent, alcohol, Betadine surgical scrub soap, glycerin, Kodak Photo-Flo (a highly refined and expensive detergent), laundry soap flakes, mouthwash and other products too gruesome to discuss. Of all these, liquid dishwashing detergent worked about the best. I buy any kind that is biodegradable and does not have a fragrance. So, when you get your new mask home, before you use it, wash the inside and outside thoroughly with thick, warm suds. Use your fingers to scrub every square millimeter of the lenses and the skirt. Every day that you snorkel, after you come out of the water, wash your mask again with warm water and detergent, and then rinse thoroughly. Then your mask will be clean.

Defogging Solution

The next step is applying the defogger. Natural human saliva—a.k.a. spit—is the traditional defogging solution. You just spit in your mask, rub it around a little and wash it off. This was very amusing to do when I was 11 years old, but it is not very hygienic and doesn't work well, either. Moreover, if someone asks me a question about their mask and I try it on, I don't like the idea of sticking my face into a bowl of their drool.

If you choose not to use spit, then you can choose from among the myriad commercial defogging aids available. There are crèmes, drops, emollients, emulsions, oils, ointments, sprays, slurries, pastes, waxes and pre-moistened toilettes. There is even a product on the market that looks, feels and smells like pulverized oysters—ugh! Some of these preparations are clearly noxious or even dangerous. On more than one occasion during my trials, I have prepared my mask with some vile preparation according to instructions, washed it out and gone snorkeling, only to return home with my eyes burning from unnamed chemicals that leached out of the product remaining inside my mask.

So what's the best way to defog a mask? One of the best ways is to apply a very thin film of the same liquid dishwashing detergent you used to wash the mask onto the lenses and then rinse it off thoroughly in cold water. The easiest and very best solution to the defogging problem, however, is a commercial product called Sea Vision Defogger, available from the Sea Vision mask company (see the Appendix for sources). I have no family members in the Sea Vision organization, neither am I being compensated, supplied with free products or receiving juicy stock options. The stuff just works.

To prepare your mask, wash as above and allow it to dry if possible. Then spray Sea Vision on the inside of the lenses and rub it all over the lens and the skirt with your finger. Spend 20-30 seconds rubbing inside the mask to make sure you don't miss any spots. Then turn the mask over and let the defog solution dry. If your hectic snorkeling schedule does not permit you to let the mask dry before and after applying the defogger, just apply it to a damp mask. It will work nearly as well. Before you start off on your next snorkeling outing, rinse the inside of the mask briefly under the faucet and you're ready to go. Using this method usually allows me to snorkel fog-free all day long.

YOUR FINS

Equipment experts all call these appliances fins, but I often refer to them as flippers because that's what they look like. Whether you call them fins, flippers, flips or flops, these neoprene rubber duckie feet are essential to provide the motive power for snorkeling.

Initially, swimmers used a rigid, abbreviated form of fins called feet. These were convenient, widely available and the price was right. However, snorkeling requires a vigorous kick and feet do not provide much stability in the water.

I once swam with an expert who decried the use of fins as uncomfortable and unnatural. He managed to delude me for years, but I can tell you that snorkeling without fins is not snorkeling. To prove it, after you have found the perfect weight, style and design of flippers for you, try taking them off after snorkeling for an hour and kick with your feet. You will feel like a puffer fish valiantly trying to chug along with its giant body and teeny little fins.

The physics of flipping is quite straightforward. When you kick from your ankles, fins work like a Type III lever with its fulcrum attached to your ankle. The lever action allows you to have a bigger kick from a smaller motion. When you kick from your hips, fins make your legs longer so the arc of your kicks displaces more water. Note: fins work by making your legs longer, so you do not want short, stubby fins.

Fins also act like springs. When a fin bends, it stores mechanical energy and releases it when the fin straightens out. This gives you a more powerful kick.

This suggests that that the best fins would be very stiff and very straight so they could bend farther and store lots of energy. Stiff, straight fins do well for SCUBA divers who have a full range of movement in the water. However, a snorkeler's kick is much shallower and it is better to have fins that are slightly bent so that they always stay under the water. Snorkeler's fins also have to be more flexible to store energy on that short downward kick. Very flexible fins are easily bent when kicking downward, storing lots of energy to be released on the upswing. Flexible fins make you a lot more maneuverable in the water, too. So, I recommend a long, very flexible fin for snorkeling. You can find information on fin suppliers in the Appendix.

Pull-On Fins

Usually, if you go to a dive shop and identify yourself as a snorkeler, the salesperson will direct you to pull-on fins. These are one-piece neoprene rubber flip-flops with a foot pocket. You can tell these fins because they close behind your heel as opposed to dive fins that are open in the back. Pull-ons are cheap—about $25-$80—and work well enough that I have seen big-shot diving instructors wearing them. I own a pair of fancy, name-brand pull-on fins that I often use when my regular fins are wet.

However, there are some problems with pull-on fins. Most are a little too spineless and limp for my taste. Pull-on fins are usually shorter than strap-on fins, so you get less power from your kick. Pull-on fins also bend around every which way on your foot, making it harder to develop very precise control. It's too much like wearing a couple of unsliced loaves of bread on your feet. Also, you cannot wear booties with pull-on fins (see below), so if you reach the shore and pull off your fins, you may be walking bare-foot on some painfully rocky ground.

Strap-On Fins

Most professional fins are of the strap-on type. For our purposes this means, 1) they are fins for serious divers, 2) they are more durable than pull-on fins, 3) they push more water with each kick and 4) they have a wider foot pocket to make room for dive booties that you wear over your feet while you are using the fins. Generally, the top-of-the-line fins are the most gimmicky and the lower level fins are plainer in appearance. Nevertheless, I usually end up with middle-priced fins because they best meet my design criteria for snorkeling: long, flexible and simple with no extra holes, protrusions or flaps to cause trouble.

Special Features and Stupid Gimmicks

I've bought many types of fins from companies like Mares, Aqualung, TUSA and Cressi Sub and they all claim to have some design gimmick that is supposed to make their flippers better than the other guys.' These gimmicks include channels, extensions, grooves, hard spots, soft spots, hinges, ports, rails, reinforcements and ribs, all designed for marketing purposes. Some fins have bands of rigid plastic embedded in soft, flexible plastic, and others have bands of flexible plastic embedded in rigid plastic. Fins also come in a rainbow of colors to match your outfit. Frankly, after you find a pair of fins that fit, the only other important design characteristics are length and flexibility.

Quick-Release Buckles

Many manufactures tout the quick-release designs of the patented buckles that hold their straps on your feet. Now I can see how quick release would be important if your fin was stuck under a rail while a freight train was careening in your direction, but I have never felt a compelling need for speed while taking off my flippers. I find that most quick-release buckles are more trouble than they are worth. They either break at the worst possible time or break my fingers when I try to open them. These heinously stiff buckles loosen up with use, but over time, they can get so loose that they open on their own. This is a good way to lose a fin out in the middle of nowhere, where you will have to swim home with only one appendage. And if a buckle breaks, you usually have to get a new pair of fins.

I have had so many bad experiences with stiff and faulty buckles that I never use them anymore. In fact, I glue my fin buckles permanently shut. I simply put my fins on by shoving my foot into the foot pocket and pulling the back of the strap up over my heel.

Split Fins

Whenever the conversation turns to flippers, I am always asked "What about split fins?" Well, split fins have a long slit cut in the middle of the flipper, making it seem that you really have two half-fins flopping on each foot. Split-fins usually have heavy stiffeners on their outside edges and thin material in the center where the spilt is. The professed goal is to produce a spinning vortex, a torus-shaped, mini-maelstrom of water that drives you forward like a jet engine. Unfortunately, I cannot see how strapping a jet engine to your butt is of any advantage to the snorkeler, who relies on quiet, subtlety and precision to stalk the reef.

Nevertheless, I recently saw a video advertisement that was very impressive. The announcer had a deep, resonant voice and someone had drawn animated vortices whirling behind the feet of the very attractive models demonstrating the fins. So, at the urging of the storekeeper—and against my better judgment—I arranged to audition a pair of top-of-the-line, "pro-model," super deluxe, extra-expensive split fins from one of the major manufacturers.

I tried them in the water, but I never detected any vortices driving me forward like a jet engine. Furthermore, I found that the split fins were deficient in the maneuverability department. Flip-tip turns, lateral movements, light treading to stay motionless in the waves and precise weaving around rocks and through channels simply were not possible with the split fins (see Chapter 4). The experience was like going from an aquatic sports car with my regular fins to a clunky, red International Harvester tractor with the split fins. Furthermore, at the surface where snorkelers swim, the split fins were woefully inefficient. It took extra effort just to propel myself forward at a reasonable rate and by the end of the trial outing my legs were crampy and burning.

As if this were not enough, the split fins were *noisy*. At first, I thought a jackass was swimming behind me wearing baskets on his hooves. To my horror, when I turned I realized that the jackass was me, wearing split fins that were splashing water everywhere. So much for quietly exploring the reef without disturbing the fish. My conclusion: stay with straight fins that are not split and you will snorkel like a champ. If you want to improve your fins' efficiency, see Chapter 3 on fine-tuning your equipment.

Cost

There is no correlation between price and suitability of fins. The best economy in buying flippers is to get the right ones the first time. If you buy a set of stinky flips that do not work as they should, you will have to replace them and that doubles the cost.

WATER CLOTHING

The first time I went snorkeling, I wore a nice swimming suit. At the end of the day, I emerged from the water with my back and neck as red and hot as a firecracker. After that, I wore a long-sleeved tee shirt with my swimming suit. This kept my back, neck and arms protected but allowed second-degree burns to develop on the back of my legs. Nevertheless, I lathered on suntan lotion and the suit and tee-shirt strategy served me well for years. When the water was cold, I pulled on a pair of my old jeans. This kept me warmer and I built up giant calf muscles resisting the drag caused by these swollen cotton fabrics in the water. Here's a tip: if you are midway between sizes, buy tees that are one size smaller because they stretch and balloon out in the water. I still keep some long-sleeved tees around and use them if my other gear is wet. If I had never tried nylon clothing, I would probably be wearing them still.

Whenever a new material is developed, promoters try to make clothing out of it. Before rubber became the province of tires, Mr. Goodyear tried to get consumers to wear rubber pants, coats, suspenders and rubber undies. In the 1960s, I saw a lot of rayon, which is made from cellulose/paper pulp. In the 1970s, there was a rash of lightweight polyester that became the butt of society's jokes. After that, "all natural cotton" made its appearance. PS: Is there *unnatural* cotton? Where does it come from—unnatural cotton plants?

For years, I laughed at synthetic fabrics. Now I am going to promote nylon clothing to you. Nylon is lightweight, very strong and dries quickly. If you are on a trip to a warm, sticky climate, or if you spend a lot of time underwater, nylon is tops. After I discovered nylon, I bought nylon tee shirts and heisted nylon pants from running stores and cross-country ski shops. They were terrific because they were sun proof, had little or no drag in the water and dried fast enough to wear them back in the water the same day. Now, every dive shop and most sport stores carry a full range of nylon clothing to wear under water.

Dive Skins

Dive skins are slippery, stretchy clothes made of nylon and Lycra that fit tight to your body. Some dive skins substitute polyester for nylon, but these are more likely to tear if you accidentally grind them against a sharp coral edge. When people talk about dive skins, they usually mean body suits that cover you from neck to ankles with a long zipper up the front, but you can also buy separate tops and trousers and they are often cheaper. The only problem with wearing a separate top and pant is that cold water can leak in around your middle.

The virtues of nylon skins are legion. They protect you from sunburn and consequently make you less vulnerable to skin cancer. Dive skins provide an important barrier to jellyfish and other floating stingers, and if you snorkel anywhere with jellyfish, this can be worth the price of admission. Nylon dive skins also provide protection from the stings of fire coral. Although the fabric is thin, I have had many brushes against potentially painful fire coral without being stung or tearing the material.

Dive skins also protect you from the cold. Although the thin material of a nylon skin will not block the cold of arctic waves, it helps hold in the warmth of your body, and wearing a dive skin can make the difference between a cold snorkeling trip and a comfortable one. At the beginning of a snorkeling session, the dive skin cushions the shock of entering cold water and helps your body adapt quickly to the temperature of the waves. At the end of the day, when your body temperature has dropped and you are vulnerable to being chilled, the dive skin helps keep you warm until you are out of the water and into some dry clothes.

Dive skins can also become camouflage and/or a fashion statement, depending on your outlook. The first dive skin I bought was from a major dive supplier, and it fit like a glove. The fabric was mostly polyester dyed blue and black, and because it was the only pair they had, I bought them. Unfortunately, after a couple seasons of snorkeling, this dive skin began fading irregularly until I looked like a snorkeling ragman. Eventually, my first dive skin wore out and I cast a bit further in my choices for a replacement. I found an online source of dive skins in a wealth of designs that cost no more than my original fader cost but looked far better. Despite scorching sunlight and salty water, none of these nylon skins has faded in the slightest (see the Appendix for sources). My latest dive skin is a grey on black nylon/Lycra seaweed design that makes other snorkelers envious and makes me invisible to the fish below. At least I hope it does.

Wetsuits

Wetsuits and their dark brethren are the type of water clothing you are most likely to see. Wetsuits are basically a sheet of neoprene foam rubber covered on the inside with some slippery fabric. This neoprene comes in a variety of thicknesses from one-eighth inch to three-quarters of an inch to suit the temperature. Neoprene foam is porous and it absorbs water like a sponge. It is this absorbent quality that gives rise to the name wetsuit, because you go into the ocean surrounded by a curtain of bubbles displaced from the wetsuit and you step back onto the land carrying a suit full of water that weighs a ton.

The primary purpose of wetsuits is to warm divers in the cold depths of the ocean. Encumbered as they are by tank and diving gear, these suits work just fine for SCUBA divers. However, it is a different kettle of fish for the snorkeler. For example, the suit is incredibly buoyant and you feel like you are wearing a big marshmallow. It is also hell to get into one of these stiff, close-fitting suits and it is worse to get them off. No kidding, you better have someone on hand to help you get your suit off the first time. I spent many solitary hours trying to disencumber myself from my first wetsuit.

Nevertheless, if you want to brave the frigid water, you will have to buy a wetsuit. Because of the popularity of SCUBA diving, you will have a marvelous variety of wetsuits to choose from. You can buy thin tropical ones, thick Arctic models, separate tops and trousers, full body suits, short-sleeved body suits, sleeveless body suits, full legs with straps (Farmer Johns), shortie torso suits and probably wetsuits to fit your cat and dog for all I know. If you are fashion-conscious, you can even buy suits in decorator colors.

I have owned and used full and shortie suits for snorkeling and I find them to be serviceable. They are warming and certainly handy if you should brush up against fire coral. However, if you can get by with a dive skin, you will be more comfortable. Note: for those of you with muscular necks, wetsuits may be too constricting. I have a neck like a bulldog and after a long session in a wetsuit, I feel as if I have been hung from a gibbet.

Dive Booties

Booties are the greatest invention for snorkelers since the facemask. They are like shoes that fit inside your strap-on fins. Booties solve the ongoing problem of what to wear on your feet while you are walking to and from your snorkeling site. If you are snorkeling above a coral reef, the sand at the entrance to the water will probably contain glassy shards of sharp coral, which can slice a naked foot to ribbons. If you wear tennies, then you have to take them off and leave them on the shore where they can easily be appropriated by young children or monkeys. Leaving your shoes also means that you will have to return to the place where you started when you are done with your snorkeling. If you are taking a boat out to the snorkel site, you will have to leave them in the boat and hope that those two soakers will be there when your boat comes back to get you. After you get out of the water, if your shoes are still there, they will inevitably be filled with water, sand and debris, which is annoying and makes it feel like you are walking in shoes lined with sandpaper.

If you purchase dive booties that are sturdy enough, you can trek through the jungle and climb over rocks, gravel and sharp coral until you find that fabulous snorkeling site your buddy recommended over breakfast. When you arrive at your destination, you can walk right into the water and put on your fins in comfort. At the end of the day, you can take off your fins in the water, stand up and walk away without slipping on those slimy rocks and bruising your pride. If you wish, you can keep walking into town and grab a burger without changing footwear.

If you have cold feet, booties will keep your toes warm in or out of fins, in the water or on the shore. And if you should step on a black sea urchin, booties can stop the spine before it finds its way into your foot.

Booties help your fins conform to your feet and protect them from being chafed by the inside of the finny foot pocket. Your feet are better supported and you can snorkel longer. Most importantly, dive booties fill up the space between your fin and your foot with rubber, and like a big rubber band, they help you transfer energy from your legs to the fins more efficiently.

I am promoting booties because I have found that snorkelers put up a bit of resistance to spending extra money for booties and the larger, stronger fins that go with them. After all, slip-in fins are so much cheaper, simpler and easier to put on and take off. Nevertheless, if you want to use the best flippers, you'll have to wear booties.

There are many types of dive booties, and you will have to choose which types are better for you. Like sneakers, booties come in high-top and low-top styles. I prefer the high-top styles because they will not come off accidentally and they provide more even padding behind my heel so the strap does not rub through my skin. I prefer booties with zippers over pull-on booties to make it easier to get them off at the end of a snorkeling session.

The next most important bootie feature is the sole. The most minimal booties have no sole or just a thin, light strip of neoprene rubber on the bottom of the bootie. I prefer a substantial sole so I can wear the booties as a shoe. One pair of my booties has a full one-half-inch sole that looks like a basketball shoe. It works just fine. Another pair has a one-quarter-inch pad of textured neoprene rubber on the sole. It turns out that these are sturdy enough to climb coral, but I would not trust them as protection from a sea urchin. You have to make your own choice from the models available to you. No matter what you choose, make sure that your booties fit. They can be tight through the foot but they cannot cramp your toes or you will be miserable. If the booties are too loose, your foot will slip around inside them and you will lose the power connection between your foot and your fin.

Special Features and Stupid Gimmicks

I have seen many booties with thick rubber logos that are great for advertising the bootie makers but cause unnecessary friction and abrasion on your feet. Usually, I just peel them off and throw them away. In an attempt to make them lighter, I have seen booties that were so thin they were useless. I have even seen booties with an opening that separates your big toe from your other toes, like the split-toe socks made for Japanese sandals. Don't waste your time or money on this junk.

Bootie Socks

I found my first pair of bootie socks in the discount box on the floor of a dive shop. They were short, slippery tube socks made of electric pink nylon, and I had no desire to acquire them. The next year, I saw this same lonely pair of bootie socks in the same cardboard box when I visited the store again. By the third year, I was sick of seeing them, and rather than leaving them languishing in that stupid box for the next millennium, I bought them as a joke.

I was amazed when I tried them out. My feet were warmer, more cushioned and more comfortable in the water when I wore these socks inside my booties. Even better, the slippery fabric helped me slide my feet in and out of my booties like magic, even when wet. A miracle.

Now if you cannot find another cardboard box with bootie socks, you can search for them on the Internet. They may be shaped like tubes or sewn up like booties themselves. Both work the same for me. If you are not yet ready to spring for bootie socks, find a cast-off pair of nylon dress socks and wear them inside your booties. They will work just fine, but they will not be pink like mine.

YOUR SNORKEL

Flash back to a movie of your ancient ancestor being chased by a tiger. Through the grasses he runs, chest pounding and breathless, feeling the hot, fetid breath of the big cat on the back of his neck. Suddenly he comes to a water hole. Your thousand-times great grandfather uses his newly evolved cerebral cortex, and without missing a step, he ducks under the tepid water to hide. Soon, his lungs are burning for lack of oxygen, but he dare not surface for fear of betraying his presence. Pulling a hollow reed from the water, he inserts one end into his mouth and breathes through the other until the danger has passed. The snorkel is the modern equivalent of that reed.

Just to put a damper on this romantic story, I must say that I have spent many years pulling up reeds and sucking on them but I have never found a green reed that was hollow enough to breathe through. I have found old, brown reeds that are hollow, but these are usually waterlogged and just waiting to deliver a big load of bacteria-infested pond water down your lungs. So I think that the familiar scene above is quite apocryphal. If you are chased by a tiger, try climbing a tall tree. If you are lucky, the feline will get stuck and will have to be removed by the fire department, during which time you can escape.

Breathing Water

Imagine you are paddling along, minding your own business, and a pert little ocean wave breaks above your head. If the top of your snorkel were open, this wave could enter the top of your snorkel and flow right down into your mouth. Generally, this is no big deal since, unlike the Ancient Mariner, you will find that sipping a little bit of ocean from time to time is not harmful. However, if a bigger wave breaks overhead, it's possible that enough water can slide down your snork to make you gag or choke. If an even bigger wave breaks into your snorkel, water can pulse down the tube directly into your lungs, which are expecting air, not water. Not only is this unpleasant, but when faced with lack of air, many people panic, flail around, drop their expensive cameras and look absurd. None of this for you, I say. Here's a basic rule of life to remember: don't feed water to your lungs.

At first, I used a simple, J-shaped tube with nothing to keep the water out. When a wave splashed water down my snorkel tube, I just blew out a lungful of air and forced the water back out the top in a maneuver called the "whale spout." When I dove under water, I remembered to keep some air in my lungs to blow the water out of my snorkel when I reached the surface. Despite the wealth of fancy snorkel devices, I still resort to the whale spout technique to clear my snorkel when necessary.

However, progress marches onward and snorkel manufacturers have developed new technology to clear your snorkel in the form of a purge valve. You will find the purge valve at the lowest point of your snorkel if it has one. The purge valve is basically a hole in your snorkel fronted by a thin piece of inner tube. Stray seawater collects in the bottom of the snorkel, and when you puff hard enough, the valve opens and lets some air out, carrying the stray water with it. I recommend getting a snorkel with a purge valve.

For the most part, this device works well. However, check your prospective snorkel to make sure that the valve actually opens when you blow into the mouthpiece and does not leak water back in when it is closed. Some purge valves require too much of a puff for me and I have to grab the mouthpiece and toot into the thing like a French horn, blowing a frenzy of bubbles around my head. This sends whatever fish I was watching into paroxysms of laughter and they quickly depart the scene to tell all their friends about the funny man. At least that is where I think they go.

My advice is to get a snorkel with some simple method of keeping waves from breaking over the top and feeding your lungs seawater. There are a myriad of flashy snorkel gimmicks devoted to the task of keeping ocean water out of your snorkel, including bends, cones, floats, hinges, tubes, twists, water traps, flaps that swing around when water hits them, and holes drilled in the side of the tube that are supposed to let air in and water out. (The one-way hole is a new engineering concept to me.) None of them work very well and I suspect their intended purpose is to drive up the price of the snorkel.

Too Long, Too Short and Too Constricted

The mechanics of the snorkel require it to be short. If it were too long, your exhaled air would just collect in the tube where you would rebreathe it and eventually suffocate. As a child, I tested this by breathing through a long garden hose from the bottom of a swimming pool. To my surprise, I could not keep it up for long. The air I exhaled just stayed in the hose waiting for me to inhale it again. If you wonder if any breathing device is too long, test it by holding one end closed and breathing through the other. If you cannot push any air in or out, then the tube is short enough.

Also, avoid too-short snorks that do not come up past the back of your neck. These are popular for divers to use on the surface but they are useless for the sport of snorkeling. I think it is advantageous to get a snorkel that is as tall as possible, so that breaking waves don't splash water into your lungs. It should be positioned so that the snorkel is straight over your head when your face is looking down at the fish.

Most snorkel tubes rise over your head but I once saw an expensive model in the shape of a C. If the snorkel became fouled and you blew in the mouthpiece to clear it, all the seawater would be blown downward onto the top of your head. Unless you feel the need to wash your hair frequently with salt water, I suggest you avoid such designs.

Make sure the tube is not constricted. Before you take a snorkel home, breathe in and out of the tube vigorously to make sure that it provides a clear airway—you should feel no resistance. I surveyed snorkels for this book and found that 1 out of 10 snorkels in my area was so obstructed that I had to suck hard to get any air. Make sure that the snorkel you chose has an airway so wide that it feels like you are breathing into the air without a snorkel.

SUN PROTECTION

If you do not get anything else from reading this book, listen carefully. You must take care of your skin. Originally, suntan oil was just oil, like baby oil, that you put on your skin to "help you tan." However, after a lifetime of tanning and burning, I have personal experience with skin cancer and now I take care of my skin. I urge you to do the same.

Sun Protection and Water Clothes

The best protection against sun is a solid, opaque barrier. If you wear a nylon dive skin that covers your upper and lower body, you only leave a few bare spots that require the use of sunblock. This is what I prefer for snorkeling. In a pinch, you can put on long-sleeved tee shirts, light pants or even blue jeans to control your sun exposure. Unfortunately, people are much more likely to do this *after* they have received a bad sunburn, rather than before.

Sunblock: Study the Label

Wherever your own skin is not covered from the sun, you must use sunblock. I remember the first suntan oil I ever bought; it had an SPF level of 5. Now that we know that ultraviolet rays cause skin cancer and premature aging, you should use a sunblock product designed to screen out the sun's harmful rays completely. I am currently using a sunscreen with an SPF of 70.

The SPF numbers on the sunscreen container tell you how well the sunscreen will protect you against ultraviolet B rays (UVB) —these are the rays that cause your skin to burn. Here is how to crack the SPF code: for the average person in bright sun, multiply the SPF number by 10 to find the number of minutes you can stay in the sun without burning. For example, if you have a sunscreen with an SPF of 12, you can probably stay out in the sun for 120 minutes or 2 hours without burning. Try to stick with an SPF over 30.

However, the SPF number does not tell you whether the contents will block ultraviolet A rays (UVA)—these are the rays that cause skin cancer, premature aging, skin deterioration, collagen damage and depletion of vitamin A from the skin. To get a sunscreen that blocks these dangerous rays, look for the code words words "broad spectrum" on the package. A sunblock that does not guarantee protection against both ultraviolet A and B rays is useless to prevent your skin from damage.

Some far-thinking sunscreen brands may mention UVA protection on the label. UVA numbers 1-4 indicate low, medium, high or very high levels of UVA protection, respectively. But usually you'll have to figure out the properties of sunscreens from the wording on the label

The Magic of Zinc

The best sunscreens contain UVA blocking ingredients such as zinc oxide, titanium oxide, avobenzone and ecamsule. I like to stick with sunblock products containing zinc oxide. Zinc oxide is the white gooey stuff that you can sometimes see on the noses of lifeguards. When it is incorporated into a crème or lotion, the result is pretty transparent and gives you sun protection without making you look like a zombie. If you are not sure whether a product contains zinc oxide, look on the label or call a general physician and/or dermatology specialist and ask what products they recommend. I advise you to use zinc oxide or titanium oxide sunblock on your exposed skin at all times, whether you are in the water or not, so you do not damage your skin and wake up one morning to find you have a complexion like scraped toast.

If you are far from home and unable to locate a suitable sunscreen, consider buying a tube of pure zinc oxide ointment at the drug store to tide you over. Ask the pharmacist if you cannot find it. Rub zinc oxide ointment into your skin until it forms a thin haze. There is no need to put it on in big, white, gooey globs.

How to Put on Sunscreen

On the Shore

Begin the day by putting on a layer of sunscreen. One of the biggest problems is getting the sunscreen preparation evenly on your skin without leaving bare spots. Start by wetting the skin of your arms with water from the faucet. Squirt or squeeze the suntan crème or lotion into the palm of your hand and rub it easily onto your moistened skin. The sunscreen will spread more evenly on wet skin and it will seal in moisture to keep your skin from drying out during the day. If the sunscreen is too thick to spread easily, mix it with some water in the palm of your hand before applying. Then repeat this procedure for all the other areas of your body that will be exposed to the sun.

Unless you are wearing cover-up clothing or a dive skin, expect to apply about an ounce of sunblock to protect your entire exposed body. There is no point in skimping on sunscreen. A thicker coat gives you more protection and lasts longer than a thin one. If the first product you try feels too greasy, gummy or never seems to dry, find another.

Allow the sunscreen to dry thoroughly before going out in the sun. Recognize that the period from 11:00 am through 2:00 pm is usually the worst time for ultraviolet rays. Be prepared to increase the thickness of your application if you return at the end of the day and find that your skin is pink or inflamed.

There are certain areas of the skin that are most often missed. Do not forget to apply sunscreen to the back of your hands, your ears and any thinning scalp on the back of your head. If you are wearing shorts, the back of your calves will present itself to the sun as you walk, so be sure to have extra sunscreen there. If you are wearing sandals, make sure there is sunscreen on the tops of your feet as this skin is often thin and tender.

In the Water

Unfortunately, when you are in the midst of snorkeling, most sunscreens just wash off. In order to get a sunscreen that stays on in the water, you need to look for the words "water resistant" (which is warranted to stay on for at least 40 minutes under water), or "very water resistant" (which is guaranteed to stay on for 80 minutes under water). I use an 80-minute product, myself. If I want to snorkel longer, I have to reapply it every hour and twenty minutes.

In other countries, you may not find the labeling as helpful, and in any case, you do not have to believe what the sunblock bottle says. The best way to evaluate your sunblock is to give it a test. Rub a generous amount onto the skin of your arm, let it dry and then rinse it under running water from the faucet. If you can still feel the sunblock in place, put it on the rest of your exposed skin and go out into the sun. If the washed-off place does not tan or burn you can continue using your regular sunblock under water.

Make sure to apply plenty of sunblock and allow it to dry before you go in the water. Make sure that every area of exposed skin is protected. If you are not wearing a top, get help from someone else to cover your back evenly with sunblock. You can never get even coverage if you try to do it by yourself. If you are traveling alone, you can ask any fellow snorkeler or even a passing stranger to help you. Sometimes the sunblock ritual can be an opportunity to meet people and start new friendships.

If you are wearing water clothes, make sure that you apply sunblock liberally to the back of your ears and neck. Rub sunblock over the areas of your face that are not covered by your mask. Cover exposed ankles and make sure you include the backs of your hands. Then wash the insides of your hands thoroughly.

Sunblock/Bug Repellant Combos

Please resist the urge to buy products that claim to block ultraviolet rays *and* repel mosquitoes and other flying insects. If you need both, buy two products and apply the sunscreen first to ensure the best skin protection. The insect repellant may last a long time but you will have to reapply the sunscreen every few hours.

Sunblock Perils

This leads us to the ongoing problem of spreading sunblock goo. Sunblock is designed to resist washing off which means it clings tenaciously to your fingers, where you can easily transfer the goo to the inside of your mask, undoing all your cleaning and defogging. If sunblock gets under your mask, it can contaminate your mask, getting into your eyes and burning like crazy. If sunscreen goo gets on your snorkel, you will taste it throughout your trip and if it clings to your flipper straps, it can make them slippery. To minimize these perils, I put on sunblock last. Then I wash my hands and wipe them with a towel before stepping out the door to snorkel.

SUNGLASSES TO PROTECT YOUR EYES

There are a number of reasons to wear sunglasses. The eyes do not like to be exposed to incredibly bright light for long periods of time. Prolonged exposure blanches the pigments of the eyes so that you will have the Dickens of a time seeing at night, so be careful driving. The skin of your eyelids and around your eyes is very sensitive and it is a bummer of a place to have skin cancer. The solution is to wear sunglasses.

Currently, the fashion in Southern California is to wear expensive fashion sunglasses. If your sunglasses cost less than your car, then you can look forward to being treated like a social outcast. However, no matter how much you spend on your Gucci's or Poochies, a high price will not guarantee safety for your eyes.

What I want from sunglasses is a tough, coated polycarbonate lens that blocks 100% of all ultraviolet rays. I want a tough frame that will not bend or break even if I sit on my sunglasses in the airplane. I want a lens that is not too light or dark and does not impart any color to my vision. Do you think this is already too much to ask? Well, I also want a pair of sunglasses that not only will not break, but will also protect my eyes from any moving particle or projectile short of a bullet! And I don't want to spend more than $20 a pair.

Surprisingly enough, there are plenty of such sunglasses available for prices that range from reasonable to nominal. They are sold as industrial safety glasses.

Yes, I remember when laboratory safety glasses were green plastic horrors that made you look like Dr. Cyclops. But modern safety glasses are made in a bunch of snazzy styles. Virtually all of them offer 100% protection from ultraviolet rays. They are usually sold with clear polycarbonate lenses but most lines also include glasses tinted to a neutral 40% grey that provides sun protection without altering natural color. It is easy to find pairs with unbreakable frames, and of course, with lenses that are licensed to protect your eyes from flying particles. Many come with wrap around lenses that protect the side of your eyes from UV and particles as well. The current pair I am using also floats.

Now that you know what to look for, you will see safety glasses being worn as sunglasses all over. For example, the last time I looked, all the players on my favorite baseball team were wearing them. To order these glasses direct from industrial suppliers, see the Appendix.

YOUR WATCH

I think that it is useful to have the kind of watch that has a rotating ring around the outside of the dial so that you can keep track of the time you started snorkeling. When you get into the water, twist the ring until the dot lines up with the minute hand. Then, when you wonder how long you have been in the water, you can glance at the watch and compare the minute hand to the dot to find out.

That being said, I do not think that snorkelers need any special type of watch. The ring feature is common on watches of all styles and prices. As long as the watch is waterproof down to 10 feet or 3 meters, it will give good service while you are snorkeling. Last year, as a joke, I wore a $19 orange plastic watch every minute I was underwater and it worked fine. SCUBA divers need giant, expensive computer watches in order to measure all manner of things—and impress their buddies—but snorkelers can wear the same watch in and out of the water.

FOR NEWBIES

If all this outlay for gear sounds like too big a deal for your first or second experience in casual snorkeling, then forget it entirely. Before you leave on your trip, if you want to buy something, buy the cheapest mask that really fits your face. All the rest of the gear is negotiable. If you find out that you don't care for snorkeling, then you've saved a wad of dollars that you can spend on something else if you wish.

You can get away with a minimum amount of gear if you are just trying snorkeling out. If you are staying at a resort or dive center, plan on renting your fins and snorkel or just borrowing them for free. Those of us who roam the water are a friendly and helpful bunch. If you strike up an acquaintanceship with any snorkelers or divers on the plane or at the resort and bemoan the fact that you have no gear, they will probably either lend you theirs or rustle some up from somebody else. On my first snorkeling trip, a near-stranger pressed me to take an expensive mask, fins, snorkel and shortie wetsuit, just because he wanted me to have fun snorkeling.

Having perfect equipment accounts for 10-15% of the enjoyment of snorkeling, at most. When you are in the mood for buying gear, you'll want to get the kind that best suits your needs. But now, just relax and have some fun. Snorkeling is all about fun, not equipment.

CARING FOR YOUR EQUIPMENT

After every snorkel excursion, wash your mask, fins, snorkel, booties and water clothing in warm, soapy water. I just get in the shower and wash my equipment and myself, every time. After washing, put defog solution on the inside of your mask and let it dry for your next snorkel outing. Hang or drape your dive skin and equipment outside to dry, but keep it out of direct sunlight. Turn your booties upside down so they drain or you will be at risk for the horrible fungal infection called "dead foot disease" (see Chapter 12). Label all your equipment with your name and telephone number. A Sharpie pen does nicely on light-colored plastic.

CHAPTER 3

FINE TUNING YOUR GEAR:

WHY PAYING THE MOST WON'T GET YOU THE BEST

I am always amused by the people who say, "You get what you pay for." This phrase is most often heard in a situation where someone thinks he paid too much for a piece of equipment and is trying to justify his purchase to you and to himself. After several years of careful thought and experimentation, it is clear to me now that the best gear is the stuff that fits best and suits your style of snorkeling. The only way to obtain this balance is to fine-tune your equipment to suit you.

FINE TUNING YOUR MASK

I use a low-volume, mask with a wide field of view, color correction and my glasses prescription ground into the lenses. The mask I have now is only better than my first $20 mask because it fits my personal needs better, not because it is more costly or has more gimmicky features.

One of the biggest mask problems is that snorkelers cinch up the straps too tight. This is painful and it leaves a fiery red ring around your face, making you look like a sewer snoid. To get the right mask pressure, you need to fine-tune your mask strap.

Place your mask on your face without the strap and inhale just enough so the mask doesn't fall off. This gives you a rough idea of the minimum pressure needed to keep the water out. Next, try the strap on your head and see if it is tighter or looser than it needs to be. Usually it will be tighter.

Now adjust the strap so that it produces a pressure about equal to the pressure needed to hold your mask on without a strap. When this is done, check to see if the left and right side straps are even. You can do this by counting the lugs or measuring the free end of the strap from the tip to the buckle. If the sides are uneven, make them equal. Now your mask is adjusted to the least amount of strap pressure necessary to keep the mask from leaking. When you get into the water, you may still wish to make fine adjustments to the strap pressure to suit your taste. The rule is: use as little strap pressure as possible to keep water from entering your mask.

Neoprene Pads and Straps

There are numerous mask strap accessories, but I will discuss just two. The first is a neoprene foam pad that fits over your strap separating it from your head. The functions of this pad are: 1) to keep your hair from tangling and being ripped out by the sticky silicone mask strap, 2) to make the mask more stable on your face, and 3) to make sure your mask will float if it slips out of your hands in the water.

The second accessory is like the one above but it consists of a neoprene pad attached to cloth straps that fit into your mask and completely replace the original strap. These cloth straps are not stretchy but they are infinitely adjustable with Velcro fasteners. This allows you to dial in exactly the right amount of mask pressure to use for the life of your mask. It also cushions your head, protects your hair, and helps your mask float in the water. Both of these products are available in a variety of colors (as if I cared).

FINE TUNING YOUR FINS

Like mask straps, it is hard to adjust your strap-on fins to the correct pressure for you. If your fin straps are too tight, they will scrunch your toes into the front of the foot pocket, which can be painful and detracts from your kicking efficiency. If the straps are too loose, you can lose a fin in the water. I remember snorkeling in deep water next to a cliff when a storm came up. I tried to take off my right fin in the water when it slipped out of my cold fingers and dropped like a stone. I put my nose into the water, kicked down as hard as I could, and I managed to catch the tip of the fin and bring it up again. I felt like Jack Paar at his pool party, diving to the very bottom of his swimming pool to retrieve his toupee before he could resurface.

To start fine-tuning, wet your dive booties, put them on your feet and slip one foot into a fin. Try to find the least strap pressure that will keep the fin from flying off when you kick your leg aggressively. Usually, this is the perfect permanent adjustment for your fin straps, but if your fins are still loose and wiggle from side-to-side on your foot, you will want to torque the strap down another notch or get smaller fins. Now, repeat this procedure with the other leg and fin. Finally, even up the straps by counting the lugs on each side or measuring the ends of the straps and tugging the straps around until the ends are equal on each side. Compare the settings on your left and right feet; they should be the same or close. If you had to tighten your straps more on one fin to keep it from moving on your foot, you may have one foot that is larger than another or you may have ended up with a pair of slightly different-sized fins. If you had to torque down the straps on both fins, make a mental note to buy fins that fit better when you have to replace these.

Adjusting Your Fins' Flexibility

The remaining fin upgrades are for both strap-on and slip-on fins. For optimum performance, your fins should bend easily in both directions. If your fins work fine, or you are hesitant to perform surgery on your flippers, stop here and leave well enough alone.

However, if your fins are too stiff, they will reduce your maneuverability and kicking efficiency and your legs will tire too quickly. If you are snorkeling with others, you will find that you are pumping your little legs as hard as you can and your friends are still way ahead of you. You will notice that you have difficulty treading water or navigating around close rocks and coral.

If you've inadvertently bought fins that are too stiff to snorkel in, don't despair. The first pair of fins I trimmed was a new pair of Cressi Subs that started out as stiff as aluminum girders. After I trimmed them, they became super-flexible and worked great. With a little trimming, you can adjust the flexibility of your present fins until they are perfect. However, this technique is a little fussy, so if you can find an old pair of fins to experiment with first, do so.

Pick up one of your fins and find the thick ridge or rib running up the left and right edges of the fin. I call these the rails. If you grab onto the edge of your fin, you will be holding a rail. These rails are the parts that control the stiffness and bendability of your fin and store energy for your propulsion. If you turn the fin over, you will see the same thick rails on the underside of the fins. Usually they are thicker toward the heel and grow thinner as they reach the fin tips. By trimming these rails, you can adjust the stiffness of your fins.

Lay your fin face down on a steady surface with the heel facing you. Start with the rail on the right side. Before cutting, remember that you should never cut toward yourself—always cut away from your body. Lean over the fin and make a cut one-eighth inch deep into the rubber of the right rail, cutting a one-eighth-inch ribbon from the heel to the tip of the fin. You should end up with a fin that has a narrow strip cut out of the right rail. Repeat the process for the left rail, then turn the fin over and cut a ribbon from the right and left sides of the sole of the fin. When you are done, all four rails should be minus a small strip of rubber.

Now, bend the fin you have just cut forward and backward and compare it to your uncut fin. It should bend more easily, and the tip should be more flexible than the heel. If your cut fin is noticeably more flexible than the uncut fin, stop. If it is not significantly bendier, take off another one-eighth-inch strip all around and try again. After you are done with one fin, repeat the process with the uncut fin.

Now put the fins on your feet and go snorkeling. If you like the way your fins work, then you are done. If you can see that the extra flexibility is helpful but you think you would like a little more bend, take your fins back home, dry them off and repeat your first session, cutting off another one-eighth-inch strip on every rail. Now try them out again. Keep making these adjustments until the springiness is perfectly tuned for you.

As you are bending and testing your fin's flexibility, you might find that it bends more easily in one direction than another. Or you may want to make it a little more flexible at the tip than the heel. All these conditions can be corrected. Just go slowly and test the fin between cuts.

Cutting Strategies

Unless you are a genius with a knife, your first cut will probably skitter around and come out of the rail after a few inches, or it may not cut anything at all. Don't worry if your cuts are not perfect. It's not that critical. Take as many small cuts as you need to remove the equivalent of a one-eighth-inch strip the length of the rail. When you are done, your work will likely be uneven. If you like, you can try to even up your rail by making more cuts, but do not become carried away and cut off too much.

In devising this technique, I tried a variety of cutting implements, including Exacto knives, German carving knives, Japanese wood marking knives and Swiss Army Knives. I came away with the realization that you should never use a clasp knife for cutting unless it can be locked open. If you do not believe me, the next time we meet I'll show you the scar where a Swiss Army knife collapsed and neatly cut off the tip of my thumb.

I did find a cutting implement that will make your job safer. It is called a cheese cutter and it consists of a broad, flat, blunt blade like a spatula with a sharpened groove cut into the center. You can use this tool to pare thin slivers of plastic from the rails of a too-stiff fin just like you would cut a wafer-thin slice from a rind of cheese. However, to work well, the cutting edge must be sharp. If you cannot find a cheese cutter that is sharp enough, you will have to use a knife. I recommend a very sharp, stiff knife that is easy to control.

Note: please be careful. Fin material is tricky to trim and it is easy to cut yourself. If you are not a DIYer, find someone who is and make them do the cutting.

Example: Mares Modification

To help clarify this method, I bought an inexpensive pair of Mares slip-on fins. They consisted of just a neoprene boot attached to a flat, clear plastic paddle blade with slim rails on all the edges. Once I got them home, I started by bending the fins in my hands to get a sense of their stiffness. I compared this to my most-perfect strap-on fins at the time made by Aqua Lung. My goal was to make the flexibility of the cheap Mares equal to the perfect flips. I took my trusty rusty cheese cutter, started trimming at the heel and worked my way to the tip. When I completed this tuning, I took them out snorkeling and found that the cheap Mares fins now worked as well as fins costing $200, except that they were a little shorter. I still use them when my regular fins are drying or when I want to have a quick dip and don't want to bother with booties.

FINE TUNING YOUR SNORKEL

There is so little to the snorkel that you would think that there is nothing to modify. However, I have spent more time fine-tuning my snorkel than any other piece of gear. It is probably because it is the only piece of equipment that goes into my mouth.

Your Mouthpiece

I don't care for most mouthpieces because they just don't fit my mouth. Either I have to bite down so hard that I get a headache or else when I relax my mouth, they leak or fall out. Most mouthpieces seem to be shaped for lizards' mouths or have protrusions that poke me and rub my palate raw.

If this is your experience, too, start by pulling off your mouthpiece and turning it upside down. This worked so well on one snorkel that I used it that way for years.

On most snorkels your can pull the mouthpiece off and replace it entirely. Lately I have been using a SCUBA mouthpiece—you can get them at any dive shop for a nominal cost. Just pull off your original snorkel mouthpiece and jam the SCUBA mouthpiece onto the tube in its place. It sounds so simple, but in fact, you may have to wrestle with your snorkel to get the mouthpiece on and off. These SCUBA mouthpieces hold firmly in my mouth without having to clamp down like a bulldog.

I usually do not care for the angle of the mouthpiece on the snorkel, either. If it is not in the right place, it abrades my lips or starts tugging one way or the other when I move my head. At first, I boiled the bottom of my snorkel so that I could swivel the mouthpiece around to the right angle, and you can do the same. However, snorkels are cheap and when I found one with a mouthpiece that swiveled, I bought it. Then I found another cheap snorkel whose mouthpiece was connected to the main tube by a short length of flexible vinyl hose so that the mouthpiece could be turned any which way. That is the snorkel that I use the most, now.

Visibility

Make sure the top of your snorkel is brightly colored: neon yellow, orange, red or green. This is the only part of you that is visible above the water when you snorkel and it is the only thing that boats can see to keep from running over your pointy little head.

If your snorkel top is black or some dark color, make sure you modify it—this tip could save your life. Diver's flags and floats are red or orange, so you should choose these colors to tell boats that you are under the water. You can probably find some brightly colored tape at a dive shop. Now, wrap the top 3 inches of your snorkel with tape before going out in the water. Sure, silver radiator tape and silver holographic tape would probably be visible from farther away, but the sun also reflects silver light from the waves and boats cannot tell that there is a snorkeler under the reflection.

Your Snorkel Strap

There are many clips and snaps to hold your snorkel to the mask, but the best and simplest is a short strip of neoprene rubber with holes punched out at each end to form a figure 8. I have never had to buy one of these—they are so cheap that shopkeepers always give them to me for free. First, fold the figure 8 around your mask strap. Then free up the top or bottom of the snorkel tube and slide it through both holes. If you cannot remove either the mouthpiece or the top device easily, try running the snorkel under hot water. If that fails, you will have to try something else.

Even this simple strap may be overkill. In a pinch, I have held my snorkel on satisfactorily with rubber bands.

To adjust the tube, put on your mask and stick the mouthpiece of the snorkel in your mouth. Place your face down into the water looking at the bottom, in a comfortable position for snorkeling. Then tug on the snorkel, pushing it up and down and twisting it in the strap until it feels OK and does not pull on your mouth. Now go into the water and try it out.

CHAPTER 4

THE RIGHT MOVES:

GREAT SWIMMING STROKES FOR SNORKELERS

The better you can swim, the more comfort, fun and safety you will enjoy while snorkeling. However, snorkel swimming is much different than the one hundred meter Olympic race. Snorkel swimming employs a lot of floating as well as fine movements to position your body and strong strokes to get you out and back when you're done for the day.

For example, yesterday I was snorkeling in a 7-foot circle ringed with long arms of fire coral. When I found a creature I wanted to watch, I dropped my fin tips down as stabilizers and fanned my hands very slightly in the water to keep in place without scaring the shy fish away. When I wanted to move, I let the current push me toward and away from the shore, maneuvering through the coral spires with shallow flips of the tips of my fins. When the quarters were tight, I pulled my arms and legs in close to my body and twisted my torso to wiggle through narrow places. When the tide shot me too close to shore, I made a shallow 180-degree flip turn at the waist and made my way back to the deeper water. I used many strokes that you could not learn at your YMCA.

Much of snorkel swimming is small movements and nuances. Soon, you will be able to move in any direction or stop in the water by moving just your fingers, hands, arms, feet, legs or body. You will be able to swim as well in 3 feet of water as you do in 10 feet of water. You will know many ways to move in the water and swimming will become so natural that you will maneuver without thinking about it.

For example, suppose I want to turn right to look more closely at a particularly attractive tunicate worm. If I'm hanging in the water, I can just rotate the inside toe of my left fin, stirring the water so that I gently spiral to the right. If I'm being carried by a current, I can use my fins as rudders to make the turn. If there are too many close coral arms, I can pull in my knees, roll one-quarter turn in the water and then straighten out again to turn. If the water is quite shallow, even 10 inches, I can float and swirl my arms gently on the surface until I am facing the right direction. If the water is even shallower, I can inflate my lungs for flotation and rhythmically move my torso like a dolphin, gliding through the water without disturbing the plants and animals underneath.

In this chapter, you will find many different snorkel swimming strokes that you've never heard of. If you want to improve your swimming technique, just snorkel more and use these strokes.

THE FIRST LAW OF SNORKELING SAFETY: BE ABLE TO SWIM

Do not try to snorkel if you cannot swim. Some people mistakenly assume that they do not need swimming skills in order to float on the top of the water breathing through a snorkel but this is a prescription for disaster. Be sure you and every member of your snorkeling party can pass these three tests:

Snorkel Swimming Safety Tests

- ☑ Float motionless for at least 10 minutes
- ☑ Tread water in the same place with your head out of water for 5 minutes
- ☑ Swim continuously at any speed for 10 minutes without becoming exhausted

If you are not sure whether you or another member of your party can pass these tests, try them out first in a swimming pool under supervision. If these tests seem a little difficult, I advise getting a good night's rest and repeating the tests tomorrow. If you have any doubts whatsoever about someone's swimming abilities, ask a swimming instructor for help. It is not safe for you to be in the water if you cannot swim.

> **CHILDREN'S SAFETY TIPS**
>
> 1. Children must never be in water that is over their heads. If your child gets too tired, too cold or suffers a cramp in shallow water, then he or she must be able to stand up and walk to you.
>
> 2. Every child who is going into open water must be able to pass the three snorkel swimming safety tests described above. If your child cannot pass these tests, sign them up for swimming lessons. It is not safe to be near the water with a child who cannot swim. Don't let children go in the ocean if they cannot pass these tests. Period.
>
> 3. Teach your child the *stand and bob float,* the *water boatman stroke,* and the *wave rider stroke* to use if they become fatigued or become stranded in the open water.

FLOATING AND SWIMMING STROKES USED IN SNORKELING

Here are some examples of techniques that I find useful. Try them the next time you are in the water.

Floats

To snorkel, it is important to be able to float motionless in the water, both to watch the creatures of the reef without scaring them away and to have a safe way of staying afloat if some emergency transpires.

X Float

This is a good posture to lay motionless in the water while you watch the marine life or fiddle with your equipment. Like the name says, lay face down in the water and spread your arms and legs to form a giant X. If you want to stay in one spot, drop the tips of your flippers down into the water to serve as brakes. This pose will stop you dead in the water and help anchor you in place against the waves. You can float effortlessly in this position almost forever. If you get bored, turn over on your back and watch the seagulls flying overhead.

Easy Chair Float

Sit in the water as if you were sitting in a living room chair and float. This position minimizes your footprint on the surface of the water, so wind cannot blow you around and the denizens of the reef will not be disturbed by your great, gangly shadow. If the water is shallow, grab your ankles or the tips of your flippers so you will not kick up the bottom sand or mud.

Skater Float

Lie on your stomach, rest both hands in the hollow made by the small of your back and lace your fingers together. In this position, you can kick lightly to move forward or stay in one spot without disturbing the water or producing dangling shadows. If you face into the current, the *skater float* presents the minimal surface area to waves so that they cannot buffet you around. By keeping your arms from dangling in the water, you will embolden many shy organisms to come out of hiding so that you can watch them.

Coffin Float

Float face down with your arms crossed over your chest like an upside down Egyptian mummy. If you need to move in the water, keep your limbs quiet and twist your body to turn or propel yourself slowly. This position helps you remember to keep your appendages from waving around and scaring the aquatic population. You can also float like this forever if you are stranded in the water. If you lose your snorkel, just turn over and float on your back.

Stand and Bob Float

When the water is deep enough, simply stand up with your head out of the water and let your breath support you. As you breathe in, you will float higher in the water. When you breathe out, you will sink in the water until you take another breath and float up again. With this technique, you can float indefinitely in energy-saving mode. Knowing this float could save your life if you are ever stuck out in the open water.

Kicks

Think of the natural divisions of your legs: hips, thighs, knees, calves, ankles, feet and toes. Different kicks may be propelled by each of these segments and each will help you move forward in a different way.

Moving your thighs up and down with your calves, ankles and feet relaxed gives you a strong kick for covering distance quickly. A leisurely kick from the knees allows you to coast forward slowly, while a quick calf kick can propel you away from rocks or fire coral rapidly if a big wave comes in. Kicking movements with the ankles and toes are the bread and butter of reef snorkeling. These kicks are shallow so you don't scare the fish and accurate so you don't run your knees or fins onto the shallow substrate or nearby coral.

Dolphin Kick

Hold your arms and feet close to your body and bend your hips and torso in a sinuous movement. You will waggle through the water like dolphins, whales, porpoises and other cetaceans. It isn't very efficient, but it gives you plenty of time to wonder what your life would be like now if your genetic ancestors had decided to return to the water.

Scissor Kick

This is the kick used in the stroke currently called *"freestyle."* The *freestyle stroke* has an interesting history. It used to be that in swim races, "freestyle" events allowed you to swim whatever stroke you wanted, mixing up or making up your own style. Subsequently these "freestyle" races came to be dominated by a stroke called the *Australian crawl*. The *Australian crawl* was faster than other strokes at the time and as everyone in "freestyle" races adopted the *crawl*, it became known as *freestyle*. Nowadays, if you swam in a "freestyle" event and used five different strokes, the judges would think you were crazy. The moral is—what you originally thought was free often turns out not to be free at all.

Oddly enough, the *scissor kick* that has become so ubiquitous in swimming sports isn't very useful for snorkeling. It makes a big racket and kicks up the substrate something awful if you're snorkeling in shallow water (which, if you have been reading this book, you surely are). I mainly use it for covering large distances of deep water on my way to a favorite shallow snorkel site or to get home quickly for dinner.

Side Kick

Now that you know the history, I can tell you that another kick preceded the *scissor kick* in the *crawl*. If you have ever learned the *side stroke* you may remember a kick where the upper leg is brought up knee to cheek and then kicked backwards against the lower leg which is held straight in the water. Well, one of the early variations of the *Australian crawl stroke* used this *side kick*, rotating left and right to alternate sides. Not much good for speed, but it conserves energy, and with long, languid kicks, you can keep swimming for long distances.

The *side kick* is much more useful in snorkeling. You can roll over on either side to check what's happening on the surface and still keep propelling yourself through the water using the *side kick*. It's a strong, quick, shallow kick that doesn't disturb the bottom.

Frog Kick

The *frog kick* was originally taught as the motive power of the *breast stroke*. It is aptly named *frog kick*, because you draw your knees up to your chest, spread them out from the sides of your body and then extend and draw them suddenly together, like a frog. If you stay relaxed, this is another energy-saving kick that you can keep up for long distances. Don't forget to croak.

Whip Kick

If you naturally assumed that the *whip kick* resembles the leg motions used by swimming whippet hounds, you would be gravely mistaken. Rather, the *whip kick* involves drawing your knees up slightly, then suddenly extending your lower legs and drawing them together in a movement like cracking a whip. This sends a stream of water pulsing to the rear and sends you straight ahead through the water. For long distance, the power comes from the thighs, although a more precise, less powerful *whip kick* can be delivered by the calves alone. The *whip kick* is quite useful in snorkel swimming as it can be performed quietly in shallow water without disturbing the reef residents below.

Slap Kick

This is a relative of the *frog kick* and the *whip kick* that I use all the time. Extend your legs with your fins parallel to the surface. Now turn the soles of your feet toward each other and squeeze them together as if trying to slap the soles of your feet together. This produces a smooth movement that will leave you gliding through the water. The *slap kick* can be very precise and almost undetectable by other creatures. Just a little flip of the big toe is enough to drive you forward or steer you precisely. It is also a very efficient kick that you can keep up for hours if you ever want to.

Paddling with Your Arms and Hands

Cat Paddle

Although it is hardly a technique, I rely heavily on a hand movement I call the *cat paddle*. From any position, cup your palm and fingers, reach out into the water and pull your hand back as if you were a cat drawing in a string with her cupped paw. This provides just enough force to make sudden, accurate changes in direction or to keep you in one spot while floating in the surf.

Wrist Twist or Hula Paddle

Other than the greatly diverting movement of hippos' ears and bulldogs' tails, rotating or twisting is not very common in the daily movements of terrestrial mammals. Nevertheless, the *wrist twist* is the most frequent upper body propulsion movement that I use while snorkeling. It is dramatically easier to do than to explain.

Hold your arm still, extend and cup your hands and draw circles in the water with the tips of your fingers. Or try to remember the rolling movements of dancers doing the hula dance. Dig up an old copy of *Hawaii Five O* at your video museum, and look at the opening sequence if you are not familiar with this move.

The *wrist twist* will steer and propel you quite accurately and is perfectly effective in just a few feet of water, where most other swimming strokes are a wash out. I have used the *wrist twist* to propel myself for hours through a large, very shallow lagoon where I saw sights never before revealed to me. These movements will also be useful when you are trying to stay in one spot while watching the action below.

Elbow Paddle

This one is simple. Just bend your arms and gently move your elbows up and down, performing a caricature of bird flight. Don't worry, no one will notice you doing this very silly movement but it will help you hover over any area of the bottom that you want to observe.

Breast Stroke Paddle

I use the *breast stroke paddle* a lot while snorkeling. You will find that you can do the *breast stroke paddle* in just a few feet of water, propelling yourself forcefully along with minimal turbulence. Start with your hands at your sides. Push both hands forward reaching over your head and draw them back to your sides in a large arc. Your hands are cupped, pulling at the water and driving your body forward. You can use left or right arms independently for quick, powerful steering. For a smaller version, just reach forward to your shoulders and pull the water down the sides of your body in a quick, shallow movement. Cup your hands and turn them to provide the most efficient momentum.

Overhand Paddle

This is the well-known paddle used in the so-called *freestyle stroke*. Start with your right hand at your side and raise your right arm into the air over your head. Reach out, enter the water in front of your head and draw your arm back underneath you until your hand is at your side again. Now repeat with the left arm. I seldom use the *overhand paddle* because it makes too much sound and disturbance in the water.

Turns

Tip Twist Turn

This is like the *wrist twist* but with your feet. Keep your leg still and make circles in the water with the tip of your fin using the muscles of your ankle and foot. With this move, you can turn easily in any direction.

Tip Flip Turn

Here is a useful tip. One flip with the inner toe of a flip can start a glide or turn, keep you stationary against wind and wave movement and help propel you through somewhat shallow water. Just flip and glide, flip and glide.

Jackknife Turn

Again, this is easier to do than to describe. Lay face down in the water with your arms at your sides and your legs together. Turn onto your right side and bend at the waist and knees, bringing your knees up to your chest. Then, straighten out your legs and body so you are now pointed 90 degrees to the right. When done smoothly, this will turn you abruptly to the right with little water disturbance. It also works well in shallow water. Try it on the left side whenever you want to turn to the left.

Snow Angel Reverse Turn

Starting out on your stomach, sit up quickly in the water and land on your back. At the same time, spread your arms and legs and squeeze them hard into your body, as if you were making an angel in the snow. This will drive you rapidly backward to exit a cave, avoid swimming into a coral head or to break through a wave that wants to smash you into the shore. It is a quick movement, and one of the best ways I know to back out of trouble.

Energy Saving Strokes to Use when You Are Fatigued

It happens to everyone at least once. You look at your watch, realize you have been snorkeling longer than you intended, and when you start off home, you realize that you are pooped. This need not be an emergency, if there is daylight, a calm sea and you can take your time. This is the moment to employ an energy-saving stroke.

Skater Stroke

This is the position I use for traveling long distances. Lay face down in the water with your legs extended and arms close to your sides. With your legs reasonably stiff, do the *scissor kick* from the hips. Using this kick, you can propel yourself forward for long distances with little resistance in the water. If you get tired of kicking your legs up and down in the *scissor kick*, you can switch to the *frog kick*, *whip kick* or *dolphin kick* without missing a beat.

Side Stroke

Just lay on your side with your head half out of the water and do the *side kick* with your legs. At the same time, reach in front of your head and pull back under the water with your upper hand and arm. This is an efficient way to to conserve energy and cover distance when you are fatigued.

Water Boatman Stroke

When I was taught this stroke at the age of 5, it was called the *upside down breast stroke*, but now the *breast stroke* has changed and the name is inappropriate. However, if you ever have a chance to watch an insect called the water boatman in a pond or lake, you will see why the stroke must be renamed for him. The water boatman is a little beetle with a shiny, round black body who lies on his back and gaily propels himself across the water with repetitive motions of his little legs. He is possibly the funniest thing you will ever see.

For our human variant, lay on your back with your legs spread and your arms together over your head. Now pull your arms in big circles down to your sides. At the same time, straighten both legs and pull them together until they are parallel and touching. As a result, you will scoot painlessly through the water on your back. It's a fun stroke, and it is so very efficient that you could travel leisurely for hours without tiring out. If you do get tuckered, relax between strokes and coast, or better yet, take a rest floating on your back for a while and watch the clouds go by.

Wave Rider Stroke

This combination of float and stroke is really a last resort, but it may come in handy, sometime. Simply drift on your back or stomach and wait for the next wave moving toward the shore. Let yourself be carried toward the shore on the wave and then paddle and kick when the wave reverses to resist being pulled back to the ocean. The *wave rider stroke* requires little effort on your part, because the waves are pulling you half the distance. However, depending on the waves and wind, the *wave rider stroke* does not always work. If the oceangoing waves are too strong and you are still drifting away from shore, you must try something else. In the worst-case scenario, just do the *stand and bob float*, conserving your energy until someone comes to your rescue.

EXERCISES TO IMPROVE YOUR SNORKEL SWIMMING

- ☑ Try swimming only with your legs, clasping your hands together in the small of your back. Use every type of kick you know. Now make up crazy, dumb kicks that no one ever has used. Kick with your knees bent, kick with your feet and ankles only, then swivel your legs around like propellers. Now take a rest.

- ☑ Cross your legs at the ankles and swim only with your arms. Do every paddle in this book, and then invent a dozen new ones. They do not have to be practical; after all, this is just a fun exercise, not the Summer Olympics.

- ☑ Hold your arms at your sides and press your legs together, knee-to-knee and ankle-to-ankle. Now swim just using your body. You can kick both legs together like a dolphin, wriggle like a caterpillar, spiral like a corkscrew or do anything else as long as it propels you forward without spreading your arms or legs.

- ☑ Swim alternately on your left and right sides, half in and half out of water so you experience equal parts of air and ocean. Now swim forward with your mask raised just enough that you see half land, half water, and try to watch both at the same time.

- ☑ Every so often, do the *Wes roll*. Starting on your stomach, do a 360 degree barrel roll in the water, turning face up and then face down. This way you can check for craft or other snorkelers nearby, identify landmarks and check the weather without having to stop and stick your head up. If you bend your knees, you can do a *jackknife turn* in any direction after you have had your look. I'm not sure why this is so fun, but it is.

- ☑ Sit up in the water in the *easy chair float* and take a rest. Now lay back and enjoy the view.

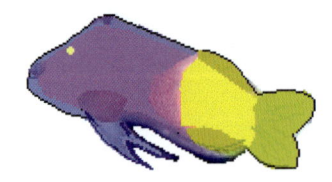

CHAPTER 5

MAKING THE PLUNGE:

WHAT TO DO WHEN YOU GET TO THE WATER

Oddly enough, getting your body in the water is the biggest barrier to snorkeling fun. If you are taking a nap, reading or watching television, it sometimes seems like it is too much trouble to get up and snorkel. If you are too tired from yesterday's exertion, too hung over from last night's partying or just bored from doing nothing, it may seem like it takes too much energy to get in the water. You can get the same feeling if it seems like the walk or drive to your snorkeling site is too long, or the sun is too hot or the water is too cold. A million pesty gripes can invade your consciousness until suddenly your mask and snorkel are in the closet gathering dust. The problem is that all these perceptions are wrong, at least for me. After the opportunity is gone, I always wish I had gone snorkeling instead of staying at home resting on my *gluteus maximus*. In contrast, I have *never* wished I had stayed at home after getting into the water. Never. So do not let inertia keep you immobile. Even if you are an experienced snorkeler, the tips in this chapter will help you fight your ennui and get back into the watery world again.

SELECTING A SNORKELING SITE

If you have been coming to the same reef to snorkel for years, you already know the best places to go. If this is you, I urge you to go back to the places you like the best. If you think you have seen everything, just look a little bit harder and you will see lots more. Or paddle on over to the next adjacent spot and look there. On the other hand, if you are new to the area, how do you make sure that you will find a fun spot to spend your day?

The first consideration is safety. All the diving books recommend that you talk to dive masters and other local residents about which sites are safe and free from wind and current. Also, find out how the wind and currents change during the day.

To discover the best snorkeling sites, start looking at home or on the plane before your arrive. Search websites, travel books and tourist information fliers to find out where the good snorkeling sites are. Look for online comments from snorkelers who have visited your destination recently and find out what sites they liked and disliked. If they identify themselves, email, chat, or text them with your questions. In the past, I have found this information invaluable.

When you get to your destination, take every opportunity to learn about the land. Buy site maps in the dive shops and look for coral formations in shallow water. Ask divers and other snorkelers for their advice on where to go.

If you run into people who are not very familiar with the sport of snorkeling, tell them you are looking for a spot where the water is calm and warm, where you can see many fish and where the depth is between 3-6 feet. If you meet some agreeable, interested parties, they may volunteer to go out with you and show you around themselves. Tell the people you meet that you are a snorkeler and they may volunteer their help. If the reefs are away from the shore, talk to boat owners about where other snorkelers have had the most fun.

Guides, Boatmasters and Groups

Take advantage of support when you can find it. See if you can find some guided snorkeling tours or groups and quiz the tour leader and participants about the best places they have found to snorkel.

If the best snorkeling is on islands or reefs away from shore, you may have to do your survey from a boat. When reefs are away from the shore, the best snorkeling is usually on the landward side of the reef. Quiet waters can sometimes be found in lagoons created by rings of reefs, mangroves or other natural barriers. Ask around to find guides or boatmasters who will take you out to the best spots on the reefs and pick you up at a predetermined time.

While my guide is taking me out, I may invite him for drinks on our return, as a subtle way of jogging his memory so that he picks me up on time.

Experienced guides will keep you in mind and will pick you up early if any problem develops. This is good insurance that you will not be stranded out on the reefs if a squall blows up or the tide goes in or out. Some of my favorite guides took me out in their boats, snorkeled with me for the afternoon and then collected me and took me home again.

I remember one time that a storm came up while I was snorkeling away from shore. My guide Hagen recognized the weather signs. He quickly gathered me up and put me back in my kayak and we started back to shore. When the wind and ocean became so rough that I had difficulty keeping up, my guide actually took my kayak in tow and paddled us both back to shore. I had a great time that day instead of a disaster.

There are some locations where the currents are so powerful that you will be carried downstream without even knowing it. It is no fun to get out of the water and find that you are far from where you started. In other places, currents are so strong that you will not be able to hover in the water and even the fish will be carried along with the current. In these locations, go with a group, a guide or a boatmaster who will keep an eye on you and pick you up downstream when you are done with your float dive.

I suspect that you will run into guides who will want to take you out to water that is 30-100 feet deep. This not the type of snorkeling experience that I advocate in this book. On this type of trip, you can spend the whole afternoon peering down into the depths hoping to see a single big turtle or a ray. Instead, I advise you to go to shallower depths where you can see hundreds or thousands of brightly colored fish and invertebrates in their natural habitat. Here you can see their behavior up close and develop an appreciation for their ecosystem. However, if you are going with a group or a tour, your choices may be limited.

Scouting Your Own Snorkeling Sites

At some point, you will want to find your own places to snorkel. See if you can find a list of potential locations in your area. Sometimes these are printed up for SCUBA divers who want to go on "shore dives." Survey potential sites by car, boat or on foot if the distances are short. When you get to your desired location, look carefully. Ideally, you should be able to see the ocean floor beneath clear, shallow water. If you can see life beneath the surface, or tide pools on the face of the reef where the tide has receded, you may have hit pay dirt. You may very well see crabs, colorful little fish, seaweed, barnacles, gastropods and bivalves. Look for the shiny reflections where the sun is bouncing off silver fish in the water. Even if you do not see a wealth of creatures at first glance, look for coral outcroppings or green seaweed on the ocean floor. These are toward the bottom of the food chain and other animals will likely be around.

Here are some bad signs to watch out for. If you cannot see anything on the ocean floor then the location is probably too deep. If the site does not have an easy way to enter and leave if you become fatigued, find somewhere else. If the sea is choppy, the waves are high or the wind is too strong, pick another site. If you are unsure whether the conditions are dangerous, watch the waves breaking against nearby rocks. Just imagine that you are the rock, and if you are going to get a beating, go on to the next site on your list. Remember, some sites that look choppy and dangerous at midday may be serene in the early morning or evening.

You may see little of interest in the waters above a clear, sandy ocean floor. Sometimes you will find sandy beaches and inlets that have been formed artificially by local resorts to attract the tourist trade. These broad, shallow areas are usually quite sterile and of little use to the snorkeler. Nevertheless, I frequently see people snorkeling back and forth in shallow water that contains nothing but sterile white sand and a few rocks. What are you looking for, people? There's nothing there!

Now go back and put on your gear. If you have selected wisely, you will have a view of paradise as soon as you enter the water.

Docks

Don't overlook the nearest dock for snorkeling possibilities. Docks are homes to little fish who like to hide during the day, bigger fish that cruise by in case some food dropped in the water, and invertebrates who like overhangs and pilings to hang onto. Even when winds blow, the sun is obscured by clouds and waves are choppy, you can see shrimp and little fish galore under protected docks.

THE RULE OF FIVE

Sometimes you will enter the water and the conditions are right but the wildlife seems a little sparse. How can you judge if this site will be worth your time and energy? I have developed a guideline called The Rule of Five to help you out in this situation. The Rule of Five states that you should be able to see at least five *different* fish species from a single vantage point if the snorkeling will be good.

Turn exactly 360 degrees and count the different types of fish you see. Even if you see hundreds of fish of a single species, they only count one for the Rule of Five. If you count five *different* species, you can usually look forward to having a great time snorkeling in the vicinity.

You can also use The Rule of Five if you are swimming down the shore and notice that the reef inhabitants seem to be thinning out. If you can no longer see five different fish from your vantage point, then consider turning back and finding another site. To improve the accuracy of the Rule of Five try looking at more than one vantage point and averaging your results.

The Rule of Five can also test your power of observation as a snorkeler. If your current site has passed The Rule of Five test, continue watching the same spot for another 60 seconds. During that time, you should usually be able to see another five completely different animal species. Some of these may be newcomers swimming by but most will be animals that you just did not see the first time.

If you are not sure whether to go to a particular location, ask your resources if it passes The Rule of Five.

TRANSPORTATION TO SHORE SNORKELING SITES

If you are snorkeling in an area where the reef comes up to the shore, then you have it made. Just walk down to a likely site and take a look at what is there. I firmly believe in staying as close to the shore as possible. If I can slip into the water without leaving the vicinity of my room, so much the better.

If I must travel to find good snorkeling, I often rent a four-wheel-drive vehicle where I can throw my wet gear—and wet self—without having to worry about where the water and sand are going. To protect the site, I always park my car in the nearest parking area and then walk the rest of the way in. Our shoreside snorkeling sites will not last long if everyone drives their car right up to the fish.

PROTECT YOUR VALUABLES WHILE YOU ARE SNORKELING

Before you leave, take a magic marker or paint stick and write your name on every piece of equipment you own. If you are staying at a resort, put this name down also. This simple step greatly enhances the likelihood that misplaced equipment will be returned and not pilfered. For example, if a local finds an expensive mask left on the dock with no indication of the owner, there is a strong urge to say "finders' keepers" and walk away with it. However, if your name is on the mask, you have created a little more personal connection with the passer-by and he is more likely to seek you out to return your property. When this happens, it is just a matter of courtesy to offer some money for the return of your property—I offer $20. This is simple politeness and also increases the likelihood that you and other snorkelers' misplaced gear will be returned in the future.

You should always query the locals about the safety of snorkeling sites. Ask specific questions, like, "Will somebody swipe my towels while I am in the water?" or, "I know that pesky kids sometimes borrow stuff, but are there any adults that cruise the beaches to steal people's gear?"

You are a bigger target when you are using a vehicle, so ask, "Can I leave my sunglasses in the car while I snorkel or will they be gone when I get back?" or, "Is there any danger that someone will steal my car, or some part of it?" Usually, the answers to these questions will be no, but you have to ask to be sure. Even if you don't have any towels or sunglasses, asking these questions will give you a sense of the local crime situation and will help you know what you do have to look out for.

The most important thing to protect is your keys. If you leave your room key around, someone will be able to get in your room. If your car key gets into the hands of passersby, you will have to walk home. If you try to hide your key under a rock at the snorkeling site, you run the risk of it being pilfered, washed away, thrown in the trash, etc. On the other hand, I used to pick such great hiding places that I could never find my keys when I exited the water. The moral is: you have to take your keys with you when you are snorkeling.

If you are a man wearing a swimsuit, there is often a key pocket you can push your keys into or a shoestring at the waist that you can tie your keys onto. However, be warned that I have lost keys from both these places. It might seem like a good idea to hang a key from a chain or thong around your neck, but these are easily caught on rocks or slide off your neck during your snorkeling gyrations. I have also lost keys that were hanging around my neck.

The solution is to tie your key on a rubber band and slip the rubber band around your wrist. Make sure that the rubber band is neither so loose that the key will fall off, nor so tight that your hand will turn blue and fall off. Then, not only is it tied to your body, but it is in front of your field of vision and you can check to make sure it is safe on the rubber band any time you like. If you do not like the thought of tying something to your wrist, then you can tie the key to the strap of your mask, where you can see it when you turn your head.

If you have a car, then you have a hiding place for small valuables. I used to hide valuables under the spare tire, next to the jack. However, in addition to being a dirty spot, it has come to my attention that in high crime areas, stealing jacks and spare tires is common. Now I take advantage of the upholstering techniques used in production vehicles. Think of the seat in your car. The cushions look thick and substantial but they are really hollow and supported by serpentine steel springs. I simply tie my valuables onto a string, reach under the seat and hook them under a loop of the springs. No one has ever thought of looking there.

ENTERING THE WATER AND RETURNING

From a Dock with Stairs

If there is a dock nearby, it is usually simpler to enter from there and swim down to your snorkeling site. If the dock has stairs, I suggest that you put on your mask and snorkel while standing on the dock, walk down the stairs carrying your fins and sit on the lowest step to put them on. Please note that, although it seems like the world's most obvious design requirement, most fin manufacturers do not make fins that float. Unless you hold them tightly, while you are struggling to put on one fin, the other will sink like a stone.

If the dock has a ladder instead of stairs, the protocol is different. Pull your mask and snorkel down over your face and let them hang around your neck. If your fins have straps, insert your wrists through them while you climb down the ladder so that your flippers will not be jostled from your grasp and fall into the water. Climb down the ladder, kick a small distance away and adopt a sitting posture in the water, like your were sitting on a chair. From this position, it should be easy to put on your fins one at a time.

Some snorkelers always want to hang onto the ladder while they adjust their mask and fins, but this is not considerate of others who want to come down the ladder behind you. If the others are energetic and anxious to get to the water, you can be caught in an annoying crush. Also, I have often seen fire coral growing on ladders just under the surface of the water and you probably do not want to start out your afternoon of snorkeling with a bad fire coral sting. So kick away from the ladder to adjust your equipment.

When you finally have your fins, mask and snorkel in place, check your wristwatch and set the timer dot over the minute hand so you can keep track of your snorkeling time.

From a Sandy Beach

I love dives that enter from the shore. If there is a sandy beach, I walk down to the water carrying my mask, snorkel and fins. Walking over the sand in my booties makes it less likely that I will break off coral or smash the living creatures that I have come all this way to see. When I reach the water's edge, I put on my mask and snorkel and then walk out until it is deep enough to sit or swim and put on my fins. This can be a little tricky, but practice makes perfect.

To some people, it seems easier to wear their fins into the water. If you prefer to put your flippers on before entering the water, either lean on the shoulder of your partner or find a clear spot to sit while you put them on. Unfortunately, once you have your flips on, it is almost impossible to walk without stepping on yourself. You could back into the water but you will not be able to see where you are going unless you screw your head around and peer over your shoulder. To avoid this, either walk with crazy-wide duck steps or take tiny sideways steps into the water. Do not be surprised if your partner doubles over with laughter. It will be his turn next.

Before you swim off, look back at where you entered and find a rock or other feature on the shore that will remind you where you entered the water. When you return, make sure you have a clear path, swim to the area in front of the landmark you memorized and stand up.

From a Shore with Big Rocks

To enter the water from a rocky shore, pick a spot where the rocks are the most shallow and even. Look into the water beyond the shore to find sandy channels that will make entering the water easier. Most people try to walk a little ways into the water until they are waist deep and then submerge.

I always try to enter the ocean without stepping on anything by launching myself into shallow water at the water line. If you want to try this, go down to the water line and look for a channel from the shore to the deeper water where you will not have to swim over a rock or anything. It need only be 12 inches wide by 8 inches deep. If there are no clear channels, pick the rock or coral spot least populated by plant and animal life. Put on your mask and snorkel, take your fins in one hand and lean over the water. Take a big breath so you are at maximum buoyancy, put your chest and face into the water, push off with your feet and slide out to deeper water.

I keep one free hand under myself so I can help my progress with a few fingers. This helps me navigate around protrusions that might otherwise scrape my own protrusions. I usually hold my fins in the other hand or park them on my back until I get free of the shore. In a few seconds, I am out in water that is deep enough to maneuver without standing or mashing into anything. Then I sit in the water and put on my fins one at a time, just like I was sitting on a sofa in the lobby of the Grand Hotel.

Some people don their fins first and then try to pick their way through the rocks wearing flippers. My advice is this—only wear your fins to climb over rocks if you want to entertain others with the sight of a fool falling on his ass. Believe me; sitting down hard and unexpectedly on a rocky reef is no picnic for your derriere.

Before you swim off, find a landmark that will help you locate the channel you came in on. Then, when you are done snorkeling and want to return to the shore, line yourself up with your reference point on shore, swim down the channel you used before, propel yourself to shallow water and stand up. You will be less likely to fall down on the rocks or sharp coral if you remove your fins immediately after standing up.

Entering the Water through Big Waves

In most cases, if there are big waves, I suggest that you find another snorkeling site. It is possible to snorkel in the face of giant waves, but it's more judicious to pick a time and place where the water is calmer and there is more to see.

You should know that there is a mythology of wave size stating that small waves come after one or more large waves. Some experts even suggest jumping into the water in the wake of the largest wave that you see, in the expectation that the next wave that comes will be teeny. Another myth perpetrated by word-of-mouth, a book and a movie, is that the ninth wave after the largest one will be even bigger and the ninth ninth wave will be a monster. My own experience suggests that this is a fairy tale.

Entering from a Steep Ledge above the Water

Once again, the safety concerns of jumping into the water from a steep ledge would seem to outweigh the relative amusement of doing so. Besides, how are you going to return to shore, by jumping *upwards* like an actor in a kung fu movie? Before you scuttle the site, look for some easier way to get down to the water on foot. I usually look for some terrestrial animals like lizards sunning themselves on the rocks near the ocean. Since lizards are not known for doing the high dive in reverse, it is an indication that it is possible to descend to the water level on foot.

Please do not dive head first in the water, unless you know for sure what is below the surface. Diving head first into water that is too shallow or has hidden rocks below the surface is the primary cause of permanent paralysis of the legs (hemiplegia) or all limbs (quadriplegia).

Entering from a Boat

The same general rationale applies if you are climbing down a ladder or lowering yourself into the water from a boat. Put on mask and snorkel around your neck, carry your fins and put everything on once you are in the water.

If you are on a big boat, you will surely see others diving into the water feet first or diving backwards into the water like actors on television. This is unnecessarily showy and will make you look like a clown. Also, if you jump into an unseen obstacle or another snorkeler there will be trouble. If the boat has a large motor, try to enter the water well away from the propellers and return the same way. You do not want to be the victim of someone else's carelessness if they inadvertently start the motor.

If the boat is small enough and everyone rushes to your side to help you into or out of the water, the combined weight may tip the boat. Instead, alert others in the boat when you are leaving and returning so they can help counterbalance you. Because of the risk of tipping in small boats, all your spare gear should be tied into the boat with rope or bungee cords before you get into the water.

Best Times to Snorkel

Most aquatic life is crepuscular. That means that the organisms are most active around dawn and dusk. Since visibility is limited in low light, it is easiest to snorkel in the morning. I usually go snorkeling in the early morning and early afternoon.

MAKING THE BEST OF A BAD SITUATION

OK. You checked with your travel guide, local maps and guides, divers, fellow snorkelers and the maid to find the best spots to snorkel and they turn out to be awful. If there is no warm, shallow, oxygenated water available to support an aquatic ecosystem, there may be nothing to see. Or if you are buffeted and crushed by the waves and angry sea, and carried away by currents so strong that you cannot stay motionless in the water, you may be out of luck.

Before you give up, look for temporary weather conditions that may be causing the fish to hide. Sometimes, the sun comes out of a cloud and everybody shows up at the party. Canvas the shore area looking for shallow water or coral outcroppings where fish may gather. Make sure you are actually in the site where you want to be. For 3 years in a row, I went out to a lagoon where everybody assured me that the snorkeling was great. Every year I met with a vast expanse of mud. Finally, I trekked twice as far as everybody told me and I found a lagoon with some of the best snorkeling ever.

If you have done your due diligence and you cannot find any good snorkeling that day, take a deep breath, relax and eat some watermelon pickle. Check out the terrestrial wildlife and the wild life on the land. Take your partner to the souvenir store. Look in the dive shops for things you do not need. Find a nice spot to eat and treat yourself to a drink with an umbrella. Then try again the next day.

COASTAL AND FRESHWATER SNORKELING

I am often asked whether there is any good snorkeling on the North American continent. The answer is definitely yes. If you want to snorkel and you are landlocked, you have two choices: 1) travel to the east or west coast, or 2) snorkel in fresh water.

The Temperature Factor

Do you know the 10% law in chemistry? It states that for every 10-degree decrease in temperature, the speed of chemical reactions decreases by 10%. That means that in cold temperatures, all the physiological reactions in fish's bodies are running as slow as molasses. No wonder they are not very active. Similarly, without a bright tropical sun, even fish with distinct and attractive markings often look bleached out. When the light is dim, the fish get pale.

Except for warm ponds and shallow lakes, bodies of fresh-water can become uncomfortably cold. Even North American coastal areas in California and Florida are cold enough that you may want to wear a wetsuit or jeans and a long-sleeved tee shirt.

Coastal North America

When snorkeling on the coast, do not expect to find the density of beautifully colored fish that are visible in the Caribbean. For example, off the California coast of Catalina Island, you can expect to see many Garibaldi damselfish. These attractive fish—the official state fish of California—are colored a brilliant, glowing international orange. Like bulldogs, garibaldi damselfish sport a wrinkle above their nostrils, which gives them a pleasingly comical appearance. However, do not expect the garibaldi to be cavorting in schools or doing much more than moving slowly through the purple and pink seaweed. Even on the hottest day of the summer, the temperature is just too cold to support much activity.

Nevertheless, snorkeling is fun anywhere. I have talked with hundreds of people who have had a great time snorkeling on the North American coasts and so can you.

Snorkeling on the mainland coast is also a great way to practice your snorkeling skills. Your equipment works the same, and you can practice all your snorkeling and swimming moves to perfection on the mainland. For example, in the kelp beds around Catalina, I did lots of side swimming, *wrist turns, tip twist turns*, *Wes rolls*, *scissor kicks* and *dolphin kicks* to maneuver up, down, and sideways between the floating strings of kelp. I think the pinnipeds who watched me (mainly seals and sea lions) were quite impressed.

Finding Coastal Snorkeling Locations

Get on the Internet, talk to your friends and get the best recommendations for snorkeling locations on the mainland coast. Select some spots that are inexpensive and close. After all, cost and convenience are two of the main advantages of mainland coastal snorkeling.

Freshwater Snorkeling Locations

If you want to snorkel but don't relish a trip to the coast, then you can snorkel in fresh water. The United States Great Lakes seem as enormous as oceans from your vantage point on the shore and the country is peppered with smaller lakes and ponds that you can try.

Ponds

Ponds are really my favorite freshwater snorkeling sites. They are usually so warm in the summer that you can snorkel easily in a bathing suit. The shallow, warm water ensures that ponds are teeming with life.

You can see schooling fish, flounder and other Pisceans. You will probably find that invertebrates are among the most entertaining creatures to watch. As a boy, I remember being fascinated by crayfish—arthropods related to shrimp and lobsters—inhabiting a pond. Insects such as water striders, water boatmen, water bugs and others are likely to be skating and swimming about. There are spiders that live underwater, building webs they fill with air to breathe. With immatures living underneath the water and adults flitting through the air above, dragonflies and damselflies go about their business as they have for the last 150 million years.

Even smaller organisms are quite entertaining. Ponds are wonderful breeding grounds for Protista, single-celled organisms whose anatomical structure and behavior is fascinating to watch. When you have become tuckered out with snorkeling and playing in the pond, take a tiny sample of pond water and put it under a microscope and you will see creatures like *Amoeba, Paramecium, Volvox, Rotifer* and others cavorting endlessly. Search the Internet for a small, inexpensive hand-held microscope if you do not have one around the house. I purchased mine from eBay. If you twiddle with the light source, you can get these transparent creatures to show up white on a jet-black background. Breathtaking. When you are done, take the remaining creatures and their water and return them to the pond so that, like Roman Viscniak, you can set an example of compassion for the lives of all creatures.

Lowland Lakes

Overall, lakes and reservoirs can be marvelous places for freshwater snorkeling. There are many lakes in relatively untrodden country where you can observe nature undisturbed by human hands. There may be fish and other shore life to explore and lakes may attract a variety of small wildlife. Try looking in the early hours for creatures who are active at night (nocturnal) or active at dawn and dusk (diurnal).

Even heavily trafficked lakes may have shores that are uncrowded and little traveled. In lakes that are used for sports and fishing, snorkelers must always be on the lookout for fishing boats, speedboats, water skiers and others who will not expect to run into a snorkeler on the surface of the lake.

Lake temperature can pose a challenge for snorkelers. Unlike Caribbean shores surrounded by bathtub-warm water, large bodies of fresh water can be too chilly to stay in for long, even in summer. This problem can be partially solved by wearing heavy clothes while snorkeling or by investing in a neoprene rubber wetsuit. Heavy winds and storms can make snorkeling difficult or dangerous on lakes. Better to avoid snorkeling at these times and wait until the weather is clear again.

Man-made lakes are sometimes choked with underwater obstacles such as trees and even automobiles that have been pushed into the lake or were around before the area was flooded. These and the detritus that becomes lodged in them can reduce visibility and provide a hazard to swimmers and snorkelers.

Some lakes are ghastly polluted and/or contain toxins. For example, it used to be amusing to swim in Utah's Great Salt Lake, where your body is so buoyant that you seem to be reclining on the very surface. Unfortunately, parts of the Great Salt Lake are now so polluted with trash and dead fish that they are difficult to drive by, much less to enter the water.

High Altitude Lakes

High altitude mountain lakes are often pristine with clear blue waters. Unfortunately, lakes that are pristine are also usually sterile. Temperature is usually the culprit. Mountain lakes are often crystal-clear because it is too cold for anything to grow in them, and without vegetation, there will be no life for you to observe.

Pools Fed by Rivers and Streams

Calm pools formed by rivers and streams can provide much to look at under and above the water. The best undisturbed pools are usually located in secluded areas, so be prepared to stick your gear in a backpack and take a hike. Beware of rapidly flowing rivers, where dangers from getting caught on unexpected underwater obstructions, dragged over rocks and dumped over falls can appear so quickly that you cannot avoid them.

Quarries, Flooded Valleys and Dams

In general, I do not recommend swimming in these places because there are so many medical cases of injury associated with them. There may be underwater obstructions, broken glass, sharp metal and poor visibility that help contribute to abrasions, cuts and injuries which can then becoming infected from bacterial contamination. Moreover, the water from some quarries contains toxins and pollutants. Some of these areas are prohibited to swimmers and divers. However, every quarry is different and you will have to use your own best caution and good judgment.

TAKE RESPONSIBILITY FOR YOUR SNORKELING SITE

Whether you pick a spot in the ocean or in fresh water, be a good example for snorkelers and swimmers who will visit the site after you. Remember that others will model their behavior on what they see you have done. When they see a littered and damaged site, they will think that it is OK for them to do the same.

- ☑ Be considerate of others when you enter and leave a snorkeling site. Park your vehicle well away from the shore and walk in carefully. You would not like it if you entered a site where the scenery has been disturbed by prior visitors who damaged trees and plants, moved rocks, and so forth.

- ☑ Never leave anything behind at a snorkeling site. Sites often become the final resting place of towels, suntan lotion bottles and equipment that snorkelers and swimmers have lost or accidentally left behind. Be responsible and take a bit of someone else's junk away with you. It isn't hard to grab a bottle, can or other piece of abandoned detritus before you leave a site. Try to take out more than you brought in.

- ☑ Never bring glass bottles or metal cans onto the shore or into a snorkeling site. This nonbiodegradable trash stays around forever. It is annoying to be walking through broken glass, discarded cans, toilet paper and filth, and it destroys the natural beauty of a snorkeling site. Broken glass and sharp can edges are hazards for adults, children, dogs and wild animals. The only sure way to avoid ruining snorkeling sites with bottles and cans is never to bring them.

- ☑ Never build a fire on the beach or shore. This destroys habitat, kills animals and plants, befouls the air and leaves a messy, carbonaceous residue that will dirty peoples' bodies, clothes and equipment for many years afterwards. If you want to cook a meal, bring Sterno or a portable stove made for backpackers. These stoves are tiny, lightweight, clean, efficient and leave no trace behind.

- ☑ Never drink alcohol at or near snorkeling sites. The shore is no place for disinhibited behavior. As a snorkeler, you want to enhance your mental clarity and amplify your awareness of the natural world around you. If you are in a group, try to avoid hanging around the site talking loudly and carousing; this detracts from the peaceful nature of the spot and may interfere with others' enjoyment.

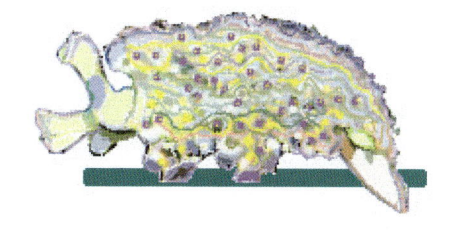

CHAPTER 6

THE REEF HABITAT:

WHAT TO SEE AND HOW TO SEE IT

Snorkeling is God's own marine ecology course and it's an experience you won't want to miss. Understanding how the trio of reef, water and animal species work together will add immeasurably to your snorkeling experience. Once you know what you are looking at, you will see more life in the ocean than ever before and you will remember more of what you see.

More important than just learning the names of the denizens of the reef, you must discover why the reef animals look and behave the way they do to get the most enjoyment from seeing them. Irrespective of anything you may have studied in school, you will begin to understand biology, ecology and the roots of social behavior in a new way when they are played out before you in real life. When you understand the reef ecosystem, you will be able to explain what you saw to others and continue the tradition of handing down wisdom from one snorkeler to the next. At the same time, you will have learned how to share ocean reef habitats with their residents without intruding into their natural cycles or generally mucking everything up for everyone. At this point, you become part of the green solution, instead of just being an outside observer.

A BRIEF INTRODUCTION TO REEF CREATURES

First off, you should realize that, unlike the land, virtually all the living things in the ocean are animals. There are few plants in the ocean. Let this sink in for a moment as you look at the outdoor world around you, right now. Unless you live in an extremely cold or dry location, you are surrounded by plants of all types and sizes. On the land, we are dependent on plants for oxygen and food. But plants are largely absent in the ocean. Even giant, green things like kelp are not true plants but rather giant colonies of algae. The basis of life in the ocean; the bottom rung of the food chain, are tiny animals made up of one or more cells, called plankton. So when we talk about ocean life, we are talking about animal life.

Help! I'm an Ectotherm

With an exception of a few marine mammals, such as whales and dolphins, the vast majority of animals in the ocean are cold blooded. Because the term "cold blooded" sounds so, uh, cold, we call creatures that get their warmth from outside of themselves ectotherms and we call animals whose body warmth comes from within themselves endotherms.

Endotherms like us generate our own body heat through chemical reactions in our bodies. When we eat, most people assume that the calories we consume are spent on keeping us moving, exercising and repairing our body tissue. In fact, the bulk of the food we consume goes to generate heat to keep us warm. This has enormous implications. Warm-blooded mammals like us must constantly stoke the fires of our body heat and so all activities are subsumed under the aegis of *keeping warm*. First off, we and our fellow warm-blooders must spend a disproportionate amount of our time eating, to keep up our body temperatures. Our lives revolve around food—finding it and consuming it.

To help clarify this point, let us take a well-known animal example, generally representative of the typical mammal. Consider the humble rat, known scientifically as *Rattus*. She wakes in the evening, she hustles across vast distances to locate food, she chows down and she races back home before morning. Our rat is very busy finding food because she must maintain her body temperature. In addition to eating, her other activities of finding shelter, building a nest, and caring for pups also revolve around this theme of keeping warm.

As humans, we spend much of our lives acquiring income that we use to buy essentials such as food, homes, clothes, beds, blankets and other items to keep us and our families warm. Proper care and rearing of our babies is virtually analogous to the task of feeding them and maintaining their body warmth. As a species, we could survive without fancy digital telephones but we could not survive without the essentials of food and warmth.

Human life and our society are dominated by the need to keep warm. Take a look at the trendy magazines at the grocery store checkout stand—my ultimate measure of contemporary culture. Every issue has articles on home cooking, restaurants, and food to feed our inner fires. These magazines are filled with popular articles about the clothing and homes that warm the celebritous and how we can attain them for ourselves. The most intimate of human endeavors are discussed in a lexicon of temperature: hot cars, hot fashion designs and hot sex. Humans are driven by the need to find *warmth*. It is a part of our vernacular, a synonym for nurturance, affiliation, fealty and all that is uniquely good and human.

Let's compare this typical mammalian picture to a different terrestrial animal that does not have to generate body heat. Think of the daily life of a young green iguana lizard, known by zoologists as *Iguana delicatissima*. This green bejeweled beauty rises in the morning, and like most cold-blooded creatures, she spends the day basking in the sun, soaking up enough heat to be active throughout the day. Although she can travel quickly to avoid predators and she can even swim through ocean waters, she will spend most of her time sitting quietly on a rock or perched in a tree. If flies happen to appear in front of her nose, she will snap them up, but she has no need of racing frantically around the geography every day searching for sustenance like the warm-bloods. She does not have to because she's an ectotherm. As she sunbathes, she spends her time in social pursuits—she clusters near other iguanas and leisurely watches them, stakes out a partner, mates and reproduces, with lots more time spent relaxing and sunning. She does not even have to care for her offspring. She just shoves her eggs into a burrow in sand or soil where they can bask in the sun, grow and wait.

Thus, for cold-blooded ocean creatures, social activities are more important than eating. When you observe them, they may appear to be doing little by mammalian standards but they are spending their energy maintaining proximity to others, swimming in schools, clearing territories, making nests, courting, mating and often caring for young.

THE SOCIAL LIFE OF FISH

One of the things that humans do that defines our species is to form groups. We naturally form couples, families, villages and towns. Many other animals have social groups and aquatic animals are no exception. Congregations of fish are usually called schools. Schooling is a very common, successful social strategy for fish and you will see fish schools every time you snorkel.

The simplest form of fish aggregation is loose groups where fish are close enough together for you to see that they are a group, but their arrangement and orientation toward each other appears random. This is often called facultative schooling. When I did a study measuring the position of every fish in a group with time-lapse photography, I found that the fish maintained remarkably consistent distances between one another, indicating that their behavior is not random after all.

Small schools usually contain about 2-10 members who swim more or less parallel to each other, enough so that you can tell that they are a school and not just a random collection of fish. These small schools swim around together or hide in a group from predators. For example, you may find a small school under the cover of overhanging rocks or docks. The group's direction is determined by consensus. If several leading members turn in the same direction, the others often, but not always, follow, and the school turns. Other times, one or two fish turn and break away from the group, cruising around by themselves before returning to the small school.

Even in a small school, you can tell that the fish all maintain consistent distance and orientation toward the other fish in the group. If you look down at a school from above, you will see that everyone is pointed in the same direction and moving at the same speed, much like flocking birds flying together in a V. However, if you look from the side, you will see that schooling fish do not swim at each other's sides but are oriented in a three-dimensional crystal lattice separated by predictable distances and angles of orientation, like carbon atoms in a diamond.

You will also encounter large schools containing thousands of fish swimming together near the shore. Inside these large schools, fish swim in unison, veering and turning together as if with one mind.

If you like, you can swim along with schools, turning and weaving in unison with the fish. It will give you some idea of what the experience of schooling is like. It's easy to get the hang of going with the group—we are social animals, after all. If the fish dive deep, I usually follow along on the surface, but sometimes I drop down under the water to swim closer with my school.

YOU CAN SCHOOL WITH THE FISH

I spent this morning schooling with a small group of 10 blue tang fish. When the little school swam by, I stayed on the surface and tagged along. After a few minutes, the school accepted my presence and appeared to ignore me. As I was swimming, I tried to focus on all 10 fish at the same time. This allowed me to gauge the school's direction and speed and made it easier for me to keep up with the movements of the group. Whenever the group turned, slowed or stopped, I followed along. When 3 of the 10 fish turned left; I followed their turn and swam with them for a short distance until we slowly veered back to the right and rejoined the remaining 7 fish. Other than keeping a watch for shallow rocks or coral that could poke me, I stopped thinking about where I was and let myself be lead by majority rule. I passed through warm spots, cold currents, bright sand and dark coves. This sort of water play makes me glad for my body, strength and coordination.

When I broke off from the school to go home, a few blue tang broke off and swam along with me. When I realized what was happening, I stopped in the water and all but one turned back to the mother school. The forward-most tang, however, just stopped in the water, looking up at me, waiting to see where we would go. I turned and headed back to the school until he rejoined his schoolmates. Then I waited until the school swam past and I turned for home again.

The Survival Advantages of Groups

Fish did not come up with the idea of swimming together on their own, nor did they learn it in school (ha). Grouping behavior evolved because fish who swim together have a better chance of survival than those who do not. In other words, the groupers lived longer and produced more offspring than the nongroupers.

Schooling confers several ecological advantages that are easy to understand. For example, just being inside a group makes you safer from predators. It's simple math. If you are swimming with four other fish and a predator shows up and eats one of you, you have a 75% chance of escaping. The likelihood of being singled out is 1/1 if you are by yourself. In a school of 1000, the likelihood of being singled out by a predator drops to 1/1000. Furthermore, fish swimming on the inside of the school, surrounded by their speciesmates, are less likely to be eaten than those swimming on the outside of the group.

Each fish in a school also benefits from the alertness of the other fish. It only takes one fish to spot a predator. If you happen to be eating and not paying attention when a bigger fish swims near, other fish in the school will spot him and you can all run away together. If you are traveling in a school of 1000 fish, your ability to detect predators could increase by 1000 times. The same advantages occur in the detection of food. If you are in a school and your neighbor detects food then you will be led to it also.

Territorial Behavior

You are bound to see some fish sitting on rocks or coral all by themselves. Although it appears that they are solitary, they are probably territorial fish in a group that maintains a large distance between members. You may see them chasing other fish away from the rock or sandy area where they are hovering, or you may see them keeping other fish away from a hiding place. This behavior of chasing other fish away is called territorial behavior.

However, don't assume that the use of the romantic-sounding word "territory" means that territorial fish are like human cowboys guarding their ranch against the outlaws. Unfortunately, the fish haven't seen any of those movies. If you observe a territorial fish like the blenny, you will find how poorly the concept fits the real world. Except for possible hiding places, there isn't anything of much interest inside most blennies' territories to guard. Most have to go off the territory to find food. Biologists often speculate that the male with the biggest, most aggressively defended territory is most likely to find a mate. However, blennies' little territories are about the same size. Furthermore, if a blenny runs too far from his spot and his hiding place is appropriated by another blenny, he does not camp outside and lay siege to his ranch. After one or two attempts, he just moves in on another nearby blenny and displaces him. This displaced blenny moves down the line and displaces someone else and so forth until everybody has a satisfactory location again.

It is said that females pick the strongest mates by analyzing the size and quality of their territories, but it is not clear that blennies spend any time looking for the best spot and they seem to function just as well in somebody else's territory as in their own.

This reminds me of a social spider species named *Oecobius gregalis* that I discovered outside Guadalajara in central Mexico and reported in Scientific American (also discussed by Richard Dawkins, see the Appendix). Spiders are such violent and aggressive predators that they seldom live in groups because they eat each other up. Nevertheless, *Oecobius* build tiny handkerchief-shaped webs under rocks and a group may consist of 2-25 webs adjacent to one other. They appear to guard these webs like territories. However, if one spider is displaced from her web, she simply goes to her neighbor and rousts him from his web. What follows is a sequential scramble, like musical chairs, where everybody displaces their neighbor until all webs have an occupant again. Like the blenny, *Oecobius* does not seem to be protecting food resources, driving away competitors or attracting mates.

If you think about it, the construction of small, adjacent territories is as much of a system for staying together as for keeping apart. If blennies really wanted to be far from their speciesmates, they would take advantage of the huge areas of uncolonized reef that have no blennies whatsoever and we would never see two blennies near one other. I think that the small size of blennies' territories ensures their access to a hiding place, enough personal space for courting, nest building and mating, and gives them an an extra jump on predators (including speciesmates) who may try to nose in and eat their eggs and offspring. At the same time, territorial blennies stay close enough together to reap some of the advantages of grouping. Like his schooling relatives, a blenny is close enough to his other speciesmates that a predator cruising by might choose to eat his next-door neighbor instead of him. In their territories, blennies are close enough together to help warn each other of danger and to see where their neighbors find food. Adjacent small territories allow blennies the best of both worlds.

REPRODUCTION AND MATING BEHAVIOR

Some schooling fish reproduce in a casual manner. Males and females release sperm and eggs into the water together, and leave their offspring to take care of themselves. Such group spawning schools can be large and the same advantages of the schooling group also apply to the newly hatched offspring. It is common to see tiny baby fish swimming in tight groups on the reef until they mature and wander from their tiny schools.

Most fish have more complex mating rituals and you are more likely to see smaller groups or pairs swimming up and down together in the water around dusk. Males can mate many times a season and may try to accumulate several females with whom they will spawn. Books and teachers often call these courtship displays, although this term takes on lots of emotional connotations, anthropomorphic bias and cultural implications that are not helpful in understanding the behavior of fish. When I see fish engaging in complex movements and behaviors that are identical or typical for all members of a species and are probably genetically coded before birth, I simply call them stereotypic. Stereotypic mating behavior serves several functions, not the least of which is to make sure that the eggs and sperm arrive together at the same time.

This is not a problem with endotherms because we keep both eggs and sperm stowed away inside our bodies to keep them warm and there is no danger that sperm and egg will wander apart after being brought together. In fact, popular culture often speaks of human courtship rituals as a process of warming. For example, see the lyrics of the song, *Let it Snow*, *Let it Snow*, *Let it Snow*. But we digress.

The behavior of male and female fish prior to mating helps prepare both fish for reproduction, helping to trigger the females to lay eggs and the males to express sperm. Other functions served by stereotypic mating behavior are to keep the mating pair from becoming distracted and trying to eat each other, to make sure that the fertilized eggs end up in the right place—such as the nest—to keep lurking usurper males from sneaking in and depositing their ersatz sperm together with the eggs of the mating couple, and so forth.

FISH SENSES

To be able to understand and empathize with with an aquatic creature, you need to get a sense of how he perceives his world. In human terms, what is he seeing, hearing, smelling, touching and tasting? If one fish is next to another, how does he detect his neighbor? How does he recognize his food? How does he perceive his mate? What exactly does he experience?

Unfortunately, fish perceive sight, sound, smell, touch and taste much differently than we do and they possess extra senses that allow them to perceive worlds that we can only imagine. Most humans assume they understand what vision is all about. We use our vision every minute of our waking lives and it is an essential part of our civilization. For example, you have never seen anyone walking down a busy street with his eyes closed. He'd be dead in a minute.

However, if you could look through the eyes of a fish, your jaw would drop. Most fish have almost a 180-degree field of vision in each eye, for a total of almost 360 degrees of vision. Imagine if you could see everything in front of you, to the left and right, above and below you, and almost everything behind you all at once. Fish can see all their speciesmates, other fish, predators, food sources, warm spots, highly oxygenated water and shelter sites moving past constantly in every direction. The human mind cannot even hold that much information at one time.

At one World's Fair or other, I remember seeing a film that had been shot by a bank of cameras pointing in every direction. It was projected on a 360-degree screen wrapped around the circumference of a circular room. I remember feeling that this much information was useless. All I could do was whip my head around, taking in little visual samples and trying to integrate them all. Fish see and understand 360-degrees of information plus everything above and below them.

For example, fish in a school can see the position of all the other fish around them, above, below and on all sides at once. This is a big help in arranging themselves in the three-dimensional lattice pattern of a school. I did some research showing that fish in schools pay close attention to the position and orientation of *at least* five other moving speciesmates at the same time. It boggles the human mind but it is just business as usual for fish.

In addition to vision, fish can detect changes in water pressure, movement, a wide range of chemicals dissolved in the water, and both magnetic and electrical signals traveling through the water. Much of this information is carried by a unique sensory organ called the lateral line. If you look down the side of a fish, you may see a faint line running from their gills to their tail. This is really a trough that contains a wealth of sensory receptor cells. Its length makes it unlike any of our sensors; by comparison, imagine having an eye that is 5 feet wide. Even in the dark, fish are observing their world by many overlapping sensory systems.

Fish integrate information from all their senses at the same time every moment. In addition, fish send signals to each other in the forms of visual movement, color, sounds, chemicals, magnetic energy and electrical currents. Chemicals, including amino acids and pheromones, are released from the surface of fish's skins, allowing fish to hunt prey, find mates or avoid predators.

And of course, fish smell (ha). If you can find the two paired sets of nostrils on the front of a fish's head, you will know that they lead into a canal and over a set of nerve fibers called the olfactory bulbs. They are so sensitive that fish can detect the *direction* of chemical stimuli coming from the open water. Human olfactory bulbs are huge by comparison—about the size and shape of the end of a Q-tip swab—but ours have little sensitivity.

Fish also have good taste. They may have taste buds on their faces and lips to evaluate the edibility of a food item before it reaches their mouths. Goatfish have long whiskers or barbels that are full of taste buds. They use these to rummage through the sand, tasting for food at a distance.

Although adults rarely mention it, one of the first things kids notice about fish is that they have no visible ears. Fish do not need external ear openings. Sound vibrations traveling in water pass through their bodies and directly into their inner ears. Living underwater helps improve the quality of fish's hearing because sounds carry much faster and farther in water than in air. Fish's ears are also more sensitive to low frequencies than human ears.

LEARNING TO OBSERVE

A Note on Size, Gender and Color

When we look at terrestrial animals, we frequently characterize them by size, gender and color. For example, you might say, "Look at the little boy in the red shirt." Unfortunately, size, gender and color are not so helpful for identifying the species of our marine brethren. In case you hadn't noticed, fish have no external genitalia, and most of them do not have obvious masculine or feminine shapes, so we cannot detect their gender by our usual cues. Moreover, many species including parrotfish, sea bass and wrasse can change their gender depending on the availability of mates.

When you see three fish with similar color and markings that are significantly different in size, don't assume that you are looking at father, mother and baby of the same species. Many different species have similar color and markings. Moreover, males and females of same-species fish often sport different colors at different ages. The colors and shapes of juveniles and babies are usually different from those of their parents and immature fish may go through dramatic color changes as they grow older. Developmental changes of color, shape, location and feeding habits help keep adults from competing with their offspring, protect juveniles from predators, keep resources from being depleted and provide other ecological advantages for the species.

Unfortunately, there are no general rules to predict what males, females and juveniles will look like. You just have to learn the different combinations.

How to See what Is in Front of You

As I found out in my initial training as an ethologist, there is a big difference between watching an animal and seeing what they are doing. In Sherlock Holmes stories, everyone looked at the scene of the crime but only Sherlock could really see what was happening, and he built his successful detective career upon this ability to observe. As soon as you walk into the ocean, you are a detective of sorts. It's fun to look around at the colorful creatures and enjoy the sun and refreshing water, but if this is all you do, you will quickly become bored. Then you will put your mask and flippers away in a closet somewhere to gather dust, forget the world of the ocean and take up some other short-lived hobby, like skeet shooting. So, slow down, open your eyes and observe.

You begin swimming slowly, in synchrony with the waves. You watch and listen to them crash and flow against the substrate, bringing oxygen to the living things all around you. In addition to the waves, you hear the vocalizations and noises produced by the living creatures below you. You watch for signs of movement or a flash of color signaling that something interesting is taking place. Without focusing, you are aware of everything at once, including the color of the ocean, the sunlight coming from the surface and the tiny planktonic life that is suspended in the water all around you.

In order to take in all these details and integrate them in your mind, you must clear your head of thoughts. There is no room for unnecessary mentation about work or school, what clothes you will wear at dinner or whether other people like you or not. There is no room for fantasies about romance, what team or party will win the race or what you will say when you win the Academy Award. In some ways, snorkeling is like an underwater Zen meditation.

When you spot something interesting, you stop swimming and your focus shifts. Now you linger on the surface, with your eyes glued to your target. If it moves, you move; if it is still, you endeavor to hover over it. In all ways, your body movements are spare and neither churn the water nor create great shadows on the bottom so that you do not spook your quarry. Your subject is bright and clear, because you are in shallow, sunny water, and you can see every detail of your creature's body, movement and interaction with the environment around it.

The trick to observing is taking the time. Be prepared to stay in this attentive mode for as long as it takes. If something of interest is unfurling below you, you might choose to spend 5, 10 or 15 minutes in the same spot. It takes time to see everything, and the longer you stay focused on an ocean creature, the more you will see that you did not observe before.

How to Watch a Flounder

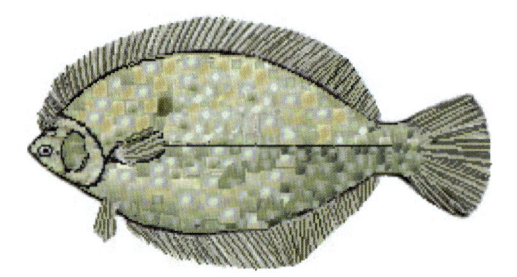

Flowery Flounder, *Bothus mancus*

Let us start our journey of observation with an animal who is as flat as a flipper. He should be easy to observe because he has only one side to watch.

Of course, I am referring to the flounder. I spot him in a shallow 5-foot pool eroded into a rocky cliff. Here, under a 20-foot rock overhang, he's stuck to the bottom while waves mix water and air and crash effervescent spew against the rocks around him, over and over. Under the cloud of bubbles, he is a handsome fellow, with round pink and pale blue polka dots spread evenly across a field of Caribbean azure. His spade-shaped body is surrounded by a skirt of pleated fins, pole green with electric neon tips. Overall, he would fit nicely on a piece of typing paper. His bright yellow eyes are set in stalks that turn backwards to peep at me. Their black horizontal-slitted pupils stare out like the amazing eyes of a goat—which are some of the most beautiful eyes you will ever see. And this is how it works: I lay in the water with my head pointed toward the flounder, my legs stretched out behind me. The tips of my fins are down in the water to anchor me as much as possible in the pounding surf. And I watch.

It is too rough to put my hands behind my back, acolyte-style, so I just flatten them at my sides and let myself be buffeted by the crashing waves. Each pull of the ocean waves sucks me away from floundie and each wave that crashes into the rocks takes me back again. I am supple, adjusting my position to the waves unconsciously while my attention is fixed on his goaty eyes, which he has locked on mine. As I float quietly for the next 5 minutes, his eyes occasionally slide away from me to look around before they quickly saccade back. Finally, I see the yellow eyes pan away from me to keep watch on more pressing matters in other directions. Now is the opportunity for which I've been waiting. Each wave that pushes me toward floundie, I take the opportunity to flip the tips of my fins slightly so I inch closer to him. Now I am passing directly over him. Wow! Now I can begin to see what he's really doing. His eyes dart around, looking for danger and food. They operate independently so he can look in two directions at once. I don't know if his eyes can see almost 360-degrees around him; if so, his visual world must be most comprehensive and exciting. I can see his gill slits open as water flows invisibly over his gill rakers. Periodically he will give an almost imperceptible shudder that floats his whole body a millimeter or so above the bottom for a moment until it settles back into the sand.

I filled a small notebook on my observations of the flowery flounder that day and yet, ultimately, my words fail me. But don't be satisfied listening to my story. Climb into the surf, locate a creature and find your own story.

Biodata

While flounders have both eyes situated on one side of the head, they are not born this way. Early in life, one eye migrates to the other side of the body so that both eyes are situated on the upward-facing side of its body. Flounders feed by hiding flat on the bottom, partially submerged in mud, and springing on their prey as it comes by. They eat worms, shrimp, crabs and small fish. Flounders are adapted to a wide range of habitats. I have seen them in the estuary outside my house and they have been found at the bottom of the Marianas Trench, the deepest location on the earth. Although they often appear on menus, their numbers are severely compromised and if you value your earth, I suggest you choose the omelet instead.

A Four-Step Checklist for Observing a Reef Creature

Here's a protocol to help you practice and improve your observational skills and begin to unravel the complex puzzle of the reef and its inhabitants. You will soon commit this list to memory so that observation and organization become an unconscious, automatic habit.

☑   *1. Where is Your Creature?*

If it swims near the surface, it may be feeding or just traveling from place to place. If it moves up and down from bottom to surface, it may be courting, laying or fertilizing eggs. If your creature stays on the substrate, does it reside in a small area on the sand, rock or coral bottom like it is guarding a territory or is it feeding on organisms on the rocks or under the sand?

☑   *2. What Is it Eating?*

There are a limited number of eating choices for animals near the shore or on the reef. Sometimes you can tell a fish's diet easily; for example, if you see her chase and eat another fish or dig in the sand, then she is a predator.

The smallest creatures—single-celled or several-celled organisms like plankton and algae—are the most important food source in the ocean. If you cannot tell what a creature is eating, rule out plankton first. What if you see a parrotfish chewing on coral rocks? You know that fish do not eat rocks, so you investigate further. Looking closer, you will see that the parrotfish has dug a little white divot out of the rock that stands in stark contrast to the darker, algae-covered area surrounding the bite. So, if the parrotfish is not eating rocks, then he must be eating algae on the rocks, right? Now we know something about the diet of parrotfish—they eat algae.

Another way of checking an organism's eating habits is to look at their mouths. For example, if you look at the parrotfish you find that he has a large, bony beak, for biting and chewing coral. The barracuda has large, prognathous, toothy jaws that are good for catching, holding and eating other fish. The Christmas tree worm's mouth is not visible but you can easily watch its two, long tree-shaped whorls. These are specialized rakes to sieve out plankton and channel them downward toward the worm's invisible mouth.

Once you find out your creature's eating habits, you know much more about its place in the ecosystem. Is its preferred food limited in supply? Does the animal compete with speciesmates or other species for its food? Does the food provide concentrated nutrition so it just has to eat occasionally or does the animal have to spend most of its time eating?

☑   *3. How Close Are its Nearest Speciesmates?*

As you have no doubt noticed, fish can be 1) solitary with no other member of the species in sight, 2) separated from each other by territories, 3) in loose groups (facultative schools), 4) in small schools or 5) in large schools. Each of these grouping patterns carries different implications for the life habits of the species and its place in the ecosystem.

Making a mental note of each fish's typical distance and orientation from speciesmates can help you better appreciate its social world. For example, silversides swim in parallel with their speciesmates, often staying about one-half to one body length away. Blue tang orient in the same direction as their mates, often staying one to two body lengths away. Blennies generally maintain a distance of not less than 3-6 body lengths from each other in adjoining territories.

☑   *4. What Is Your Animal Doing Right Now?*

Keep your eyes on a single animal, watch it and notice everything it does. This is the foremost way to gain an understanding of ocean creatures and it is the basic tool of ethology—the study of animals' behavior in their natural environment. Eventually you will develop a written or mental list of all the behaviors you are likely to see in a member of this species. If you just commit yourself to spending the time with the same animal long enough, you will begin to develop a second sense of how they spend their time and even what they will do next.

I have a group of animals that I visit almost every day. I float on the surface and watch them for 20-60 minutes at a time and I have come to understand both their species traits and their individual behavior. If you revisit a spot but you cannot locate exactly the same individuals, try to find others of the same species and size in the same area and observe them about the same time every day to get a sense of how they spend their time.

CHAPTER 7
CONGENIAL CREATURES OF THE REEF:
FASCINATING FISH AND INTERESTING INVERTEBRATES

You will make many friends on your snorkeling adventures. I hope many of them will be creatures that you find under the waves. To prepare you to make their acquaintance, here is some background information about my favorites.

Blue Tang

Blue Tang, *Acanthurus coeruleus*

Blue tang (*Acanthurus coeruleus*) are some of my favorite fish. Juveniles start with a bright, butter-yellow body with neon blue tracings on the edges of their fins and around their eyes giving the impression that they are wearing psychedelic specs. Sometimes these juveniles grow large before changing their color, so you may see bright yellow adult-sized juveniles swimming together with blue adults in schools. In between their juvenile and adult stages, tangs have a blue head and body with a bright yellow tail.

As adults, blue tang are usually about 8 inches in length, rounded in shape, and are colored a beautiful blue, which can vary from a deep cobalt to light powder blue to almost white. They have a bright yellow spine forward of their tail fin which they can use as defensive weapons against other fish. The presence of this yellow spine helps distinguish tang from other surgeonfish and doctorfish; close relatives who often mix with the tang in their schools. Blue tang adults are usually seen in small schools containing between 4-30 individuals.

Redlip Blennies

Redlip Blenny, *Ophioblennius atlanticus*

Redlip blennies (*Ophioblennius atlanticus*) are 2-4 inches in length. Their heads and bodies are chocolate brown and they sport a red line across their lower jaw that is reminiscent of a big clown smile. You can usually see redlip blennies darting back and forth, poking their heads in and out of holes they have selected or laying supine on the surface of rocks or coral. You may find that a large collection of blennies staring up at you with their goofy grins can be startling.

Males and females look similar and both maintain territories by rushing out from their resting location to chase and nip unwanted approaching fish. When space is crowded, some intruders are other blennies looking for space, and blennies who leave their own territories briefly may find a usurper there when they return.

Males clean debris from crevices to prepare nests and mating activities begin just after dawn. During mating, blennies' red lips and faces darken and females tip up at a 45-degree angle in display. Studies suggest that male and female blennies prefer large mates over smaller ones. Males approach and peck the tops of the females' heads, then both race back to their nest, where the eggs are laid and fertilized. On successive days, several females may lay their eggs in the same nest.

After fertilization, males clean the eggs, fan them to improve oxygenation and guard them from the many egg-eating predators on the reef. When the eggs hatch, the tiny fishies disperse from the nest into the oceans. Later they will settle in blenny-inhabited areas where they will form their own territories and go through the whole process again.

Fairy Basslets

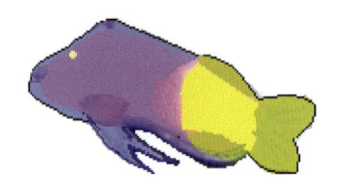

Fairy Basslet, *Gramma loreto*

Fairy basslets (*Gramma loreto*)—also known as royal gamma—are beautiful fish about 1-3 inches long, whose blue faces fade into a neon purple head and a bright lemon yellow tail. They may be found under ledges and outcroppings, sometimes swimming upside down as they feed on plankton. When approached too closely, fairy basslets dive into nearby crevasses or holes but they may come out again if you wait quietly. They usually stay near their safe-holes and chase other hole-loving species away. You will often see fairy basslets living in groups of 1-2 mature males and several females. The resident males chase away other competitive males of the same species.

The males build nests of algae within holes in the rocks and coral. Just before dawn on the day of reproduction, females enter the nests and lay their eggs, which the male then fertilizes with his sperm. Whether they rest partially inside or around the mouth of the opening, males are prepared to race into the nest to block the entrance when other fish approach. The male cares for the eggs by cleaning and fanning them to improve aeration until the tiny fish are ready to go out on their own.

French Angelfish

Juvenile French Angelfish, *Pomacanthus paru*    Adult French Angelfish

You will have no trouble seeing the 2-4-inch juvenile French angelfish (*Pomacanthus paru*) with their black bodies and striking vertical yellow stripes. Juveniles feed on algae and copepod parasites picked from other fish. They form cleaning stations where grunts, jacks, moray eels, snappers, surgeonfish and wrasse line up and wait their turn to have their skins cleaned.

Adult French angelfish have black bodies 8-12 inches long, with a liberal sprinkling of bright yellow spots that look like sunlight sparkling on the surface of a lagoon at sundown. They feed on algae, coral worms and sponges. You will usually see adult French angelfish swimming in pairs or small groups. Males and females pair up for mating and stay together for life. When it is time to spawn, pairs become strongly territorial, chasing away neighboring pairs.

Rock Beauties

Rock Beauty, *Holacanthus tricolor*

Rock beauties (*Holacanthus tricolor*) are angelfish who put on different colors according to age and reproductive cycle. Juveniles (1-4 inches long) are entirely yellow with the exception of a dark spot on their side. This dark spot is ringed with electric blue, as are their eyes.

As the juveniles age, the spots on their sides get bigger and when they reach adulthood (5-8 inches), rock beauties bodies become fully black with lighter reticulations—only their heads and tails remain bright lemon-yellow.

When it is time to mate, the rock beauty males form large territories encircling smaller female territories. Males' heads change to black, so they look like a black fish with a yellow tail. After mating, their heads change back to yellow again. If the male dies, the largest female can change sex to become a male and mate with the remaining females. Typically, rock beauties mate by releasing eggs and sperm in the water together at dusk.

Rock beauties are beautiful in any of their color morphs. They feed on algae they scrape from rocks and coral, and you will find them nibbling on sponges and other small creatures. Rock beauties are often found in and among fire coral. You will usually see them feeding or patrolling territories on rocks and reefs.

Cocoa Damselfish

Cocoa Damselfish, *Stegastes variabilis*

Juvenile cocoa damselfish (*Stegastes variabilis*) are easy to notice because of their beautiful colors—they are electric blue over neon yellow with little freckles of blue on the yellow sides of their heads. As they grow older, their upper bodies turn gray, but their gold bellies and electric blue freckles persist. Finally as adults, about 3-4 inches long, cocoa damselfish are gray fish with lighter colored bellies, and no trace of their brilliant blue or yellow color remains.

Damselfish eat algae from the surfaces of rocks and coral, as well as plankton and small shellfish. When other fish intrude into their territories, cocoa damsels erect their fins and dart at the other fish to chase them away. After fertilization, egg clusters are defended just as aggressively.

Stoplight Parrotfish

Juvenile Male and Adult Female
Stoplight Parrotfish, *Sparisoma viride*

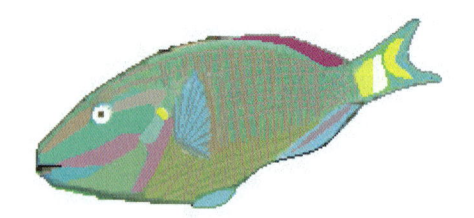

Adult Male Stoplight Parrotfish

Stoplight parrotfish (*Sparisoma viride*) display a dizzying array of color changes throughout their lifespan. The youngest males and females are violet-grey with three rows of white spots running the length of their bodies.

Adult females and immature males are usually 5-10 inches in length. They are colored bright salmon pink with a piano key arrangement of large white and black scales on their bodies. Their heads are grey with intricate, camouflagey lines and mottled shapes in light green. The light green theme of the head is repeated in a band on the tail, which is tipped with burgundy pink. Some of the females will change genders and become sexually mature males, while others will continue to grow without changing their gender or coloration.

Adult males are typically 12-18 inches in length. Parrotfish have large scales that allow for dramatic patterns of body color and texture. Their bodies are emerald green and the variations and iridescence of the body scales give the appearance of malachite. They sport violet, pink and salmon-colored markings on their heads; iris-purple and cornflower blue markings on their fins; and rows of yellow, emerald, and blue scales on their tails. The titular stoplight is a bright yellow dot on the upper sides of the gill covers.

Parrotfish have fused teeth that resemble beaks and their face markings are frozen into a perpetual smile, like a Polly who has just received her cracker. Their beaks, smiles and bright coloration contribute to their parrot moniker. Parrotfish use their beaks and strong jaw muscles to bite and scrape algae and polyps from coral. As they eat, they ingest the coral (which is composed of calcium, like limestone) and grind it within their alimentary system to free the food particles. Discarded calcium granules are released from the parrotfish's gill slits in white clouds and they drop to the bottom as sand.

Like so many animals, stoplight parrotfish are crepuscular—they are most active around sunrise and sunset. Generally, stoplight parrotfish can be seen swimming alone, although they may temporarily join loose groups of the same or different species. Parrotfish are pelagic spawners who release many, tiny, buoyant eggs into the water that float freely until settling on the bottom to hatch.

WHERE ARE ALL THE BABY FISH?

While snorkeling on the reef you may notice that you see no baby fish. Most reef fish hatch from microscopic eggs into barely visible, transparent larvae sporting spines, spikes and other protuberances from their bodies that give them a bizarre appearance. These larval fish form multispecies groups where they feed on plankton. You may find these tiny creatures under rocks or between the spines of sea urchins. Others travel great distances during the larval stage before they mature into juveniles and settle on the reef where you first observed their parents.

INTERESTING INVERTEBRATES

Any discussion of aquatic creatures would be woefully incomplete if it did not include invertebrates. Every ecosystem, in every part of the world, is dominated by invertebrates. Everywhere you look, invertebrate animals grossly outnumber vertebrates and outpace them in diversity. We are most familiar with mammals, which include ourselves, monkeys, dogs, hogs, cats, rats, mice, opossums, rabbits, cows, pigs, sheep, foxes, coyotes, wolves, elephants, giraffes, bison, oxen, rhinos, gerenuks, cheetahs, ocelots, lions, tigers and bears—oh my! Overall, there are about 5,400 different species of mammals known throughout the world. Among other common vertebrates, birds lead the pack with 10,000 different species, plus 8,000 reptile species, 5,500 amphibian species and 28,000 species of fish, totaling 58,000 different types of vertebrates.

This may seem like a lot of diversity, but within marine invertebrates, there are 250,000 different species of mollusks; 52,000 species of lobsters, shrimps and crabs; 9,000 different jellyfish and coral species; 7,000 starfish and sea cucumbers; and 5,000 sponges. If we add 25,000 flatworm species and 15,000 segmented worms, we get over *350,000* different species of common invertebrates. Even this is small potatoes compared to the insects, which number 30 *million* species. The basic message is, do not overlook the invertebrates because there are lots of them, and they are all over the place.

Invertebrates are creatures without an internal skeleton. Instead, invertebrates have their supportive skeleton outside their body, called an exoskeleton. The exoskeleton is nature's most brilliant invention. If you had a skeleton on the outside of your body, you could sustain vast crushing pressures and live through dramatic, death-dealing falls and crashes. You would immediately become a superman. Because of better leverage from muscle attachments, you would be able to lift tractor-trailers and push over high-rise buildings. Your protective outer shell would preserve you from environmental toxins and extremes of dryness and temperature, and predators would be foiled in their attempts to eat you because they could not break through your hard outer covering.

As an exoskeletal creature, there would be only one limit to your power—the engineering dynamics of an exterior shell limit your size. That is why, with notable exceptions, animals with exoskeletons are small. Being a marine invertebrate gives you a little advantage, however, because buoyancy can compensate for the effects of gravity; but for the best function, you would still want to stay less than 1 foot in size. Yes, I know that king crabs and tropical invertebrates can get much bigger, that segmented worms can grow to great lengths, and so forth, but the usual constraints of an exoskeleton keep you pretty shrimpy.

Exoskeletons are primarily made of one of two compounds. The amino acid called tyrosine is secreted by the bodies of arthropods like insects, spiders, scorpions and their brethren. When exposed to light it hardens into a shield of strong, interlinked molecules. The tyrosine system dominates the hard exoskeletons of land invertebrates. In water, exoskeletal structures are usually made of calcium, which is readily available and literally as hard as limestone. If they are small, inedible, or if they can find shelter in rocks and crevices, some marine invertebrates do without a rigid external shell altogether.

I encourage you to take a few minutes to notice how ancient, effective, and well-designed marine invertebrate body systems are compared to our clunky mammalian body designs, which have yet to survive the test of time on a global scale. Right now, vertebrates are big fish in a little pond, but compared with the invertebrates that have dominated the earth for eons, we vertebrates may turn out to be just a flash in the pan.

Overall, marine invertebrates are some of the most colorful and exciting creatures that you are likely to see while snorkeling. Many SCUBA divers are unaware of these interesting creatures because they cannot swim unobtrusively in the shallow water regions where the most interesting and colorful marine invertebrates live.

Beautiful *Elysia*

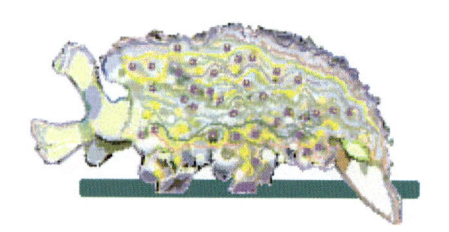

The Lettuce Sea Slug, *Elysia crispata*

Consider *Elysia,* a romantic and feminine name befitting a jewel among the most attractive of reef creatures. Her Latin name of *Elysia* is from the Egyptian word for heaven. Greeks and Romans used the word to denote the lush hillsides where the deceased would live, relaxing and dancing to the strains of the lyre, eating sweet fruit and enjoying pleasant companionship throughout eternity. *Elysia* also harkens back to the Elysian Mysteries, an ancient occult group engaged in raising human consciousness on earth. All of this is fitting to the beauty that is *Elysia* and far more appropriate for our delicate and beautiful creature than her cloddish English common name, the "lettuce sea slug"—ugh!

Elysia crispata belongs to the molluskan family of gastropods—including snails, cowries and conchs—in the order of the opisthobranchs. You will find her making her way across the surface of coral and rocks at a grand but ladylike pace. If she is really hoofing it, she might move across the rocks or bottom at about an inch per minute.

At first glance, these 1 x 1 x 3-inch beauties look like a little slip of ruffled white lace attached to the rock or sea bottom. If you take a closer look at *Elysia's* lace, you will see it is really a gathering of vertical white ruffles waving in the current, attached to the single bottom foot of the slug.

The pale ruffles can vary in color from white, yellow, sea green, aqua and blue. The most delicious *Elysia* I've seen had a salmon pink blush around the tips of her milky white ruffles which, when brushed aside by the current, revealed a beautiful band of teal blue underneath.

A pair of rolled tubes sticks out in front of *Elysia's* head like white mustachios. She uses these tubes, called rhinophores, to sniff out minute quantities of chemicals dissolved in the water. As lovely *Elysia* makes her way along the rocks or coral, she sways her head gently to and fro, gathering sensory data to guide her progress. Periodically, she stops to feed, relax, warm herself and soak up oxygen.

Elysia feeds on algae and she can release their chloroplasts into her ruffles. Thus, although she is an animal, she can participate in photosynthesis and acquire energy in the form of sugar from sunlight like a plant. Her ruffles also increase the surface area of her skin and improve her ability to extract oxygen from the water.

Elysia provides a good example of the importance of taking in all the details of the ocean in order to observe what is going on beneath you. For 3 years, I actively snorkeled the same spot looking for colorful invertebrates, but I never saw any *Elysia*. Every evening I reread my taxonomic identification books, looking at pictures of *Elysia* and her relatives, but I never recognized one. Then one day my mind made the connection and I realized that those white and green patches fluttering in the waves were *Elysia*. I had a perfect memory picture of everything I had seen on my previous snorkel outing and I was able to look back in my mind and see the *Elysia* that I had not noticed before. It was then a simple matter to step back in the water the next morning, retrace my previous swimming route and find every one of the *Elysia* that I had failed to observe the day before.

Needless to say, these creatures are not always easy to find. The key to locating *Elysia* is to locate other *Elysia*. I have frequently searched for days to find them and then located several within a few feet of each other. If you are in luck, you will locate an active sluggie that you can observe making her way across the substrate, who will lead you to others enjoying the same microenvironments.

By the way, sea hares, *Elysia*'s distant gastropodan cousin in the family Aplysiidae, have served a critical role in our understanding of the nervous system. Thanks to the tireless work of neuroscientists, *Aplysia* have the best-understood central nervous system of any animal. We know lots more about the brains of *Aplysia* than we do about yours.

Christmas Tree Worms

Christmas Tree Worms, *Spirobranchus gigantea*

Christmas tree worms (*Spirobranchus gigantea*) are segmented worms from the class called Polychaetes. Unfortunately, you will never see the body of the Christmas tree worm because he never leaves his hole in the coral. However, the part of the Christmas tree worm that you *can* see is so magnificent that it makes up for the occult nature of the worm himself.

Imagine you are a worm. As a baby you go straight to a head of coral and drill a hole big enough for your body. Then you coat the inside of the hole with a layer of calcium, making a tube in which you will live, protected from predators. Out of your head, grow three structures. The first two look like identical, marvelously detailed, feathery, spiral Christmas trees about 1 inch long. These Christmas trees can be colored pure white, yellow, orange or red. They wave like banners in the tiny microcurrents, filtering out tiny organisms and funneling them into your wormy mouth as you hide inside your tube. They also serve as respiratory organs that soak up oxygen from the nearby water. The third structure growing from your head is a little flap, called the operculum, which functions as a door to seal the top of your tube.

Feel free to enjoy the magnificence of the worms' feathery Christmas trees, but if you go too close, the worm will draw in his trees like lightening, sealing off the tube with his operculum. Unless you are watching closely, the visible parts of the worm seem to disappear in midair, following the best tradition of Harry Blackstone.

Nimble Spray Crab

Nimble Spray Crab, *Percnon gibbesi*

Once you see nimble spray crabs (*Percnon gibbesi*) in action, you will never forget their beautiful appearance and delightful behavior. Also called urchin crabs, these crustaceans average about 1 inch in width and are usually found in groups, dashing around under spiny sea urchins (see Chapter 8). Despite the striking, neon yellow color of their leg joints, when nimble spray crabs freeze, their camouflage is so perfect that they disappear from view.

If you observe nimble spray crabs for a while, their behavior pattern becomes clear. First, nimble spray crabs are actively seeking *protection* from predators. Their position underneath the black spikes of urchins, their quick movements and their ability to camouflage themselves are readily observable. Also, nimble spray crabs are continually involved in *feeding*. Their smallest pair of legs is near their mouths and you can see these small legs moving in a blur, grabbing tiny plankton from the water and tossing it into their mouths. You can also see that they are aware of their *speciesmates*. When one nimble spray crab moves, especially if it is a big one, the nearest crab changes its position, causing the crabs nearest it to adjust their position, and so on, so that the species-typical distance and orientation is maintained. When many crabs group together, you can see a ballet of interpersonal spacing unfolding under the spines of the protecting urchin.

Crabs are technically 10-legged crustaceans with tails, but this nomenclature is confusing. What you will actually see are two modified legs with claws and four pairs of walking legs sticking out from the edges of a rounded shell. You will never see the tail, which is kept tucked under the body. Their eyes are elevated on eyestalks, which allow them to move in any direction. Fish are their main predators.

Crabs are ancient creatures, dating back to the Jurassic period when they shared the seas with marine crocodiles, ichthyosaurs and plesiosaurs, and dodged the feet of giant terrestrial dinosaurs wading in the surf. There are about 6,800 different crab species in the oceans today.

Coral

Coral Polyps, *Montastrea cavernosa*

Most people who look at coral think they are seeing a big rock. However, coral are small animals of the class Anthozoa. The individual anthozoans live in colonies containing thousands of speciesmates. Each polyp resembles a tiny sea anemone a few millimeters long. Their tentacles direct food inward toward their central mouth. Each coral individual secretes a protective shell underneath and around themselves. Over time, the aggregation of these shells forms the structures that we call coral heads.

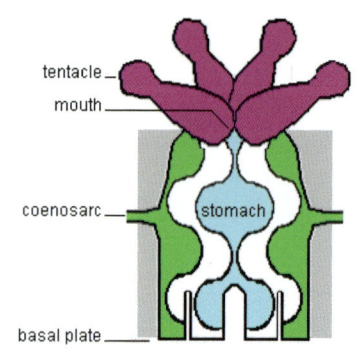

A Coral Polyp

All my life I had heard coral described as solitary animals living in shells whose walls abutted the shells of their neighbors. Then I found that coral are much more than a collection of individuals sharing the same public housing.

Each polyp is connected with its neighbors by stalks called coenosarcs that tie all the colony members together into a giant superorganism. These conduits exchange biochemicals, nutrients and algae between all colony members. They are like a vast, complex network of vessels connecting the bodies of the polyps together.

Coral colonies start from a single individual and grow by asexual division of each polyp into many identical individuals. Thus, every polyp in a colony is genetically identical to every other—they are clones. The same is true of the most evolutionarily successful social insects such as ants, and bees: colony members are genetically identical.

This is worth considering. In humans, psychologists have studied identical twins separated at birth. Despite being raised by different parents, with different families, in different socio-economic strata, in different cultures and in different countries, these identical twins were remarkably similar. For example, they combed their hair the same way, wore the same clothes, used the same cologne, had the same jobs and liked the same things. In other words, they responded in unison, despite being separated by thousands of miles.

In coral, where all individuals are identical clones, the unison of hundreds of thousands of animals challenges our understanding. Are these interconnected polyps more like a distributed colony or do they function more like an individual composed of cells, with outsourced sensory, appetitive and digestive functions? I wonder about the concept of lifespan and death in coral colonies. Does each individual polyp grow old and die, or is the whole colony more like a single organism that lives for ages? If these questions interest you, check the writings of French naturalist and philosopher Henri Fabre, who did a good job of examining such issues in the early part of the last century.

Coral work both sides of the reproductive cycle. Every polyp in a colony can reproduce asexually by dividing or budding off parts of itself to form new genetically identical clones. Coral also breed sexually by simultaneously releasing eggs and sperm into the surrounding water. This event usually takes place around the time of the full moon. Some coral colonies are a single gender while others release both eggs and sperm. The initial sexual forms are called larva or planula, which are usually pink and elliptical in shape. Each larva drifts through the ocean, feeding and growing, until it matures, attaches to the ocean floor and begins to clone a new colony.

Coral also manage to get the best of both animal and plant physiology. With their tentacles, polyps gather in floating planktonic animals as well as unicellular green algae. Then, like the beautiful *Elysia*, the coral separate the chloroplasts from the algae and transport these micronelles to their tentacles, where the chloroplasts engage in photosynthesis and capture more energy for the coral animals. This is why most coral grow in clear, shallow water where sunlight is available for photosynthesis.

Coral colonies are the heart of the coral reef habitat and they provide the environment that supports all of the animals discussed in this book. However, coral populations are being destroyed all over the world by uncaring profiteers and ignorant consumers. Do not buy pieces of coral skeletons you find for sale in rock and mineral stores, gift shop doo-dads containing pieces of coral, ground coral for calcium or other nutritional uses, or any other product that needlessly supports the destruction of these social animals. If you are not too scared, inform shop owners why you are not buying their coral products and encourage them to be compassionate and responsible for our living world by going coral-free.

Chitons

Lined chiton, *Tonicella lineata*

Chitons are common but oft-neglected marine denizens of ancient origin. They have been around since the Cambrian period, about 542 million years ago, before any animals lived on the land. The chitons of today look like their ancestors—some of whom were as large as trucks—and also resemble the ancient trilobites that are commonly found as fossils.

Early in my snorkeling years, a comrade with a boat dropped me on an offshore Puerto Rican reef to snorkel for the day. After 1-2 hours of swimming, I climbed back on the rock to rest and noticed with delight that the rock appeared to be covered with fossil trilobites. I was nearly shocked out of my skin when I touched one and it moved. Although chitons are exclusively marine animals, they can suck their shell down to the substrate and tolerate being out of the water for long periods of time.

Chitons consist of eight overlapping shell-like plates encircled by a wide border called a girdle. Most chitons spend the night crawling slowly across rocks feeding on algae. At daybreak, some return to approximately the same spot to spend the day. Most that I have seen have been 3-5 inches long, but the largest species can grow up to 1 foot in length. Their colors range from bright yellows, oranges and purples, to dark shades of green and brown that match the underlying coral rocks.

Chitons were first identified by Linnaeus in 1758. Chitons are mollusks, a group that also contains bivalve shellfish, octopuses, squid, snails and other creatures. They all possess an external or internal calcium shell.

SEA TURTLES

Green Sea Turtle, *Chelonia myda*

Sea turtles are the last living marine reptiles that roamed the seas with the dinosaurs and they have remained mostly unchanged over the last 100 million years. They are still found in every ocean except the Arctic. Like birds, their front limbs are adapted so they can fly, although sea turtles fly through the water, not the air.

Because of their specialized front legs, sea turtles are clumsy on the land and spend their life in the water except for brief forays onto dry, sandy beaches to lay eggs. When these hatch, the tiny turtles race to the sea, dive in and swim away.

Turtles evolved on the land and returned to the ocean, like dolphins, porpoises, whales and manatees—they have lungs and breathe air. Typically, green sea turtles can stay underwater for about 5 minutes before they need to surface to breathe. Turtles have exceptional vision and they can see things in the ultraviolet spectra that are invisible to humans.

Juvenile green sea turtles are omnivores that eat jellyfish and tiny crustaceans. Sea turtles are immune to the stings of box jellyfish, and they cull these pesty stingers from snorkeling waters. Because jellyfish are high in salt content, green turtles have glands near their eyes that excrete the excess salt. When they reach adulthood, green sea turtles become vegetarians, feeding on seaweed (algae), and sea grass that grow on the ocean floor. Turtles are one of the few creatures that eat sea grass and they play an important part in maintaining this habitat where many fish breed and develop.

Sea turtles have few predators other than man and can live for 80-100 years. Some studies suggest that turtles do not have programmed aging and the potential upper limit of their age may be much greater. Unfortunately, because sea turtles and their eggs are harvested for food, the adults are caught in fishing nets and the beaches where they lay their eggs are destroyed, sea turtles are seriously endangered animals.

Although everyone seems to like turtles, I find it incomprehensible that divers, snorkelers and swimmers chase them and attempt to touch them. It drives me crazy whenever I see characters on television or in the movies trying to grab onto turtles and ride them around like Ski-doos. Imagine that you are a turtle swimming under water, holding your breath, and a bigger creature grabs you from behind. You are in shock with terror and fear. You swim and swim, trying to get away, but this creature has you in a death grip. Finally, you are running out of air...

Green turtles are beautiful, gentle, venerable and vulnerable. We can show our respect by leaving them and their habitats alone. If you want to take stronger action to help turtles, see the Appendix.

OCEAN PLANTS

OK, now that we've covered many animals of the reef environment, what about all the plants? Surprise! There aren't any reef plants, or at least not very many. Unless you are sitting in a stand of eelgrass, it is likely that all the life forms around you that look like plants are really animals. So, what about that sponge, sea fan or leafy looking thing? They're all animals. What about the green stuff that looks like it has leaves? No, that is probably algae, a collection of single-celled organisms containing chloroplasts that photosynthesize. What about all this waving green seaweed? Also a collection of single-celled organisms, with no tissues, vascular system, roots or leaves. Ecosystems dominated by tall trees, bushes and grass are a land-based phenomenon. Here in the reef, almost everything you can see is an animal.

Please note: for excellent photos and information about all the marine animals mentioned in this book I recommend the books by Paul Humann and Ned DeLoach mentioned in the Appendix.

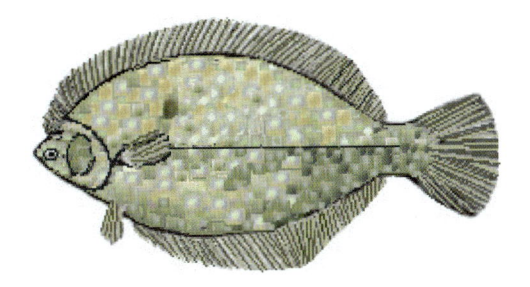

CHAPTER 8
ANIMALS TO WATCH OUT FOR:
SOME ARE DANGEROUS AND OTHERS ARE JUST MALIGNED

Instead of stressing the beauty, behavior, biology, diversity and ecology of oceanic animals, films and television programs seem only to want to scare their viewers. I frequently find that the term "ocean life" is used synonymously with "ocean terror." Nature television programs, in particular, quickly degenerate into violent, bloody and hateful diatribes about the dangers of sharks, rays, barracuda, eels, jellyfish and other supposedly deadly ocean creatures. In this chapter, I will explain why these presentations are the most irresponsible hype, are meant to scare viewers in the interest of generating income and are merely an extension of the authors' own fear of animals.

If you listen to divers brag and talk about their experiences, they really give both sides of the story. Although every diver seems to have her own personal yarn about her brush with death, you will notice that the majority of these stories are about disasters that *almost* happened. Listen for the diver who *saw* a shark, who was *followed* by a barracuda or who *almost* stepped on a ray. In fact, it is rare to run into a diver who has really been dangerously compromised by any ocean creature. According to my count, the main sources of real diving danger are: 1) problems with the dive computer, 2) problems with the regulator, 3) problems with the current, and 4) staying down too long. By comparison, the main dangers I hear snorkelers discuss are: 1) problems with the current, 2) problems with storms and tides, and 3) staying out too long. None of these potential dangers involves animals. Snorkeling is about enjoying nature and being part of it, not being scared of it.

Ocean creatures are not hostile or malevolent and they have little interest in interfering with human snorkelers. They are busy living their own lives and you are welcome to take a back seat and enjoy their experiences with them. The main animal discomforts I hear about from snorkelers are from the smallest, least threatening creatures: scrapes from brushing against coral and annoying stings from tiny jellyfish and their kin.

In the ocean as on the land, trouble seeks out those people who are careless. Consider the fellow who told me, "They said to watch out for stepping on sea urchins but I walked around barefooted anyway. I didn't think it would hurt so much. Ouch."

Others do not seem to be able to bring enough cranial capacity to the problem at hand. For example, I remember hearing this story one evening at the bar:

"Hey! I thought I saw this big fish hiding under a rock but the water was really cloudy and so I swam in really close. I was sure it was going to bite me but it swam away fast when I moved aside."

To astute snorkelers, this account leaves several important questions unanswered. Why was this man trying to intrude on a fish that was obviously trying to hide? What could he possibly expect to gain by crowding a large, unknown fish in murky water? And why was he snorkeling in cloudy water in the first place? What this yahoo was describing is a good strategy to frighten a fish into defending himself.

I have also met individuals who have the bizarre notion that they should be able to behave impulsively and inappropriately without having to pay the consequences. Imagine the woman who said, "Everybody told me that barracuda were harmless, so I tried to see if I could follow and catch one of them." This is a case where the application of a little common sense goes a long way.

Large ocean animals are really pretty kind and forgiving in comparison to large land-dwelling creatures. I knew an animal behaviorist who was an expert in the study of grizzly bears. He had trained generations of students to exercise caution and respect around these dangerous animals and he was a leader in his field. One day he forgot himself and ventured too close to a mother bear's cubs. He told me, 'She came up to me and just gave me a little cuff with her paw. Just a gentle little cuff, like she would do to her own cubs, to let me know not to hang around her babies. As a result of this tender little cuff, my friend has no face from the left side of his nose to his left ear. I'll take the dangers of the ocean any day.

"DANGEROUS" DENIZENS OF THE DEEP

All right, let us look at some of the real dangers that you will face during your day in shallow water.

The Bearded Fireworm

Bearded Fireworm, *Hermodice carunculata*

Bearded fireworms (*Hermodice carunculata*) are a joy to watch. The last one I saw was colored lime green down the middle of its back and it had bright red and white tufts along its sides. Pink, orange, lemon yellow, dark green and brown are other common colors. Fireworms have wavy appendages sticking out of their heads that look like beards. Their bodies are divided into segments and as they walk slowly along the rocks, each segment wriggles back and forth like a bulldog's butt.

You can find these wormies in crevices on reefs, although I have often seen them crawling out in the open. They are usually between 2-4 inches in length. Fireworms are annelids, just like our beloved earthworms, and they belong to the class called Polychaetes

Each segment of the worm sports a brush of white bristles. The "fire" in their name refers to the feeling on your skin if you accidentally brush against them. Some old-timers suggest that you can pull out the bristles with tape. But that doesn't matter because you're not going to touch any part of the reef with any part of your legs, arms, hands, fingers or body, ever. Right?

The Long-Spined Sea Urchin

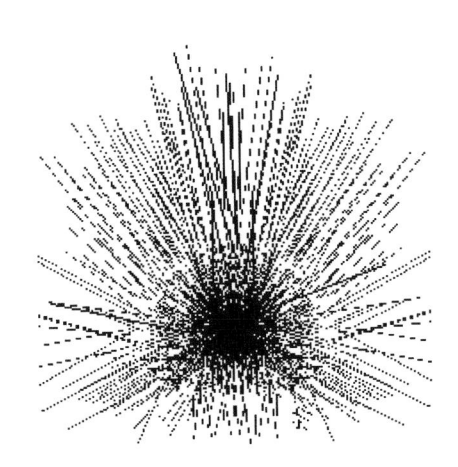

Long-spined Urchin, *Diadema antillarum*

If you swim in the Caribbean, you are likely to make the acquaintance of the long-spined sea urchin. Called *Diadema antillarum*—which means the diamond of the Antilles islands—these creatures possess 3-8-inch, thin, black, brittle calcium spines growing from their sides that make them look like big, hairy fuzz balls. If these needles penetrate your skin, they make a puncture that hurts. Invariably this happens when people step on the urchins with bare feet. As snorkelers who respect all living creatures, we never stand or walk on the bottom and never touch anything in the ocean, so there is no reason for us ever to be stuck.

Urchins like the ones we see everyday were around 450 million years ago. They were first described by the Greek philosopher Aristotle, who noted that their mouth with five-toothed jaws resembled the type of lantern Greeks kept in their homes. Ever since then, the structures of their mouths have been called Aristotle's lantern.

The long-spined urchin is an echinoderm, an ancient family that also contains sea stars, sea cucumbers and sand dollars. Unlike most of the animal kingdom, echinoderms' limbs and organs radiate from the center of their bodies. Nevertheless, they possess the basic five-pointed design that reflects the physical pattern of all higher species.

Long-spined urchins and their brethren operate by hydraulics. The pressure of fluid rhythmically directed into tube feet underneath the animals' bodies makes them scoot slowly across the ocean floor. The coordinated action of the tube feet also helps draw food items toward their mouths and can be strong enough in some species to allow them to pry a clam or other bivalve apart.

The worst that sea urchin punctures can cause is a little discomfort. School-aged children usually fare better than adults because they become busy doing other activities and just forget about the whole thing. If you think that a piece of the spine is still in your foot, it is OK to try to pull it out with a pair of tweezers. However, I have searched carefully and I have never found a spine in the punctures I have sustained by careless walking. Nevertheless, if the problem seems severe or the site becomes infected, feel free to consult a local doctor who will have seen many spines in tourists' feet and will know what to do.

What else can you do to relieve the mild, burning pain? Actually, I just ignore the thing for 10-20 minutes until I forget about it. At most, I may apply a little warm water and soap as I might to any cut or scrape. That said, there is no end of bad advice on how to treat an urchin puncture. One self-proclaimed authority says to light a candle and drip burning hot wax onto your skin until the wound is covered. That sounds like the cure is worse than the disease. Other "experts" advise applying beer, lemon juice, orange juice, tomato juice, vinegar, wine or other acidic fluids in an attempt to dissolve the calcium carbonate spine.

I remember when I was on a research trip to Puerto Rico and my doctoral professor, Peter Witt, sustained an urchin puncture. A young man, who was helpful, courteous and generally just sucking up to this famous gentleman, was anxious to be of service. "Would you like me to pee on your foot for you, sir?" he asked. Professor Witt barely raised an eyebrow. "*No*," he said solemnly, and walked on.

By the way, recent efforts at sequencing sea urchins' DNA have discovered that sea urchins and humans share similar immune system genes. Who would have thunk it?

Fire Coral

Fire Coral, *Millepora dichotoma*

Fire coral are colonial marine organisms that look rather like real coral. However, they are members of the class Hydrozoa—not Anthozoa, like true coral—and they are actually more closely related to jellyfish and stinging anemones than true coral.

Fire coral is remarkable for its fiery color and the burning sensation that it produces if you bump against it. Fire coral grows in plates and fingers on rocks and coral heads and it has a strange propensity to grow on the underwater portions of ladders and railings that you are likely to grab without thinking. When fire coral sticks out from coral heads it is easy to brush against it while swimming, causing a nasty scrape and releasing nemocysts that produce a burning sensation.

To combat this pest, just be aware of it. True to its name, fire coral is an unmistakable fiery reddish-yellow color that is hard to miss. If you keep a conscious lookout long enough, your subconscious mind will eventually take over the vigil and you will be less likely to swim near it thoughtlessly. Or else wear a dive skin that blocks the sting.

I am almost never stung by fire coral, anymore. When I do, it is usually because I have been snorkeling for too long and I have become fatigued and careless. Then it is a signal to get out of the water and go home to rest for a while.

Sea Nettles

Sea Nettle, *Chrysaora quinquecirrha*

The sea nettle jellyfish, *Chrysaora quinquecirrha,* was first identified in 1887. Jellyfish come from the phylum Cnidaria which, oddly enough, comes from the Greek word *cnidos*, which means stinging nettle. Jellyfish are closely related to corals and sea anemones.

Sea nettles are passive drifters and swim slowly by opening and closing their bells. Tentacles extending down from the bell form a trap for the plankton and tiny fish that are the sea nettle's food. Each tentacle is covered with stinging cells that are used to secure prey or for defense.

Unlike everyone else you know, sea nettles have no digestive tract, brain, heart or lungs. Instead, their central cavity serves as both heart and stomach, where nutrients are absorbed. Instead of lungs, they breathe oxygen that diffuses directly into their tissues from the surrounding water. Instead of a central brain, sea nettles have a net of connected brain cells called, appropriately enough, a nerve net, which can detect the presence of prey items directly by touch. They have small structures that detect gravity and control the pace of swimming movement. Sea nettles also have tiny eyes, called ocelli—which means tiny eyes. Ocelli can differentiate light and dark, helping the jelly to tell up from down and detect the presence of nearby prey.

Sea nettles begin as transparent larva, covered with tiny hairs called cilia that propel them through the water. Eventually, each larvae swims to a firm surface, attaches to it with a stalk and becomes a polyp. Polyps look like upside down jellyfish or tiny sea anemones, with a bell pointing up and tentacles rising toward the surface. The polyp is sexless but it can reproduce asexually by budding off segments, which then turn upside down, with bell and tentacles pointing downwards, and assume the familiar adult form of sea nettles.

Adult sea nettles reproduce sexually. Males release their sperm into the surrounding water. Then the sperm swim to a female sea nettle, enter her mouth, swim to her eggs and fertilize them.

Sea nettles reproduce logarithmically, which means that each jelly produces many offspring, and after a few generations under favorable conditions, all these offspring can quickly add up to a lot of jellies. This rapidly forming, dense population of jellies is called a bloom. Algae and other organisms that reproduce logarithmically also form blooms.

Jellies can inflict mild stings if their tentacles touch your skin. The sting comes from macroscopic little biosprings carried on the surface of the tentacles that release their points upon contact. Thus, stinging is a completely automatic reaction and indicates no hostility on the part of the jelly whatsoever. If you run into them, they cannot keep from stinging you.

I remember snorkeling in a lagoon one day when I ran into a cloud of micro jellies who stung exposed parts of my lips and face. There was a sense of both a small pinch and numbing that was startling and uncomfortable for about 30 seconds. After I realized there was nothing important wrong, the stings were gone and forgotten. However, one of my snorkeling mates reacted more strongly than I to the surprise of the mild stings. As per my advice, she was swimming in shallow water, so she could have just stood up momentarily but she stayed in the water and was stung some more. Subsequently she made her way back to shore and sat out the remaining minutes of the snorkel excursion on a dock.

The thing that makes stinging coelenterates most annoying is that you really cannot see them in the water because they are usually quite transparent. Even if you saw one, you would probably have no way of knowing whether it was a species that was stinging or harmless. The only sure way to know that stinging jellies are around is to be stung by one.

If you are stung in the water, the most important thing to remember is not to panic. It is definitely disconcerting to be stung by something you cannot see but the pain is much less than being stung by driver ants, velvet ants, honeybees, bumblebees or other serious stingers. When I feel a sting, I usually change course and swim somewhere else. However, I have frequently received one or two little stings, kept on snorkeling in the same direction, and never felt anything else the rest of the day. If you run into more than one or two stings, especially in quiet waters, I suggest that you just stand up and change snorkeling sites.

Dive skins and other water clothing can protect against jelly stings, so if you have reports of jellyfish in the neighborhood, cover up. I have heard that coating your own skin with Vaseline will fend off stings, but this sounds like an abhorrent greasy mess to me. On the other hand, it seems like covering exposed skin in SPF 70 sunblock is along the same lines, helps prevent skin cancer and seems less onerous. Sunblock gets all over everything in creation, anyway.

What can you do to ameliorate the discomfort of the mild sting? While in the water, I always rub the stung area with my fingers. Jelly stinger experts repudiate this behavior but I do it anyway. Once on shore, I have seen other swimmers trying to deaminate the sting with acids like vinegar or orange juice. I have also seen them applying topical cortisone and antihistamine crème or taking oral antihistamines like Benadryl. I just take a hot, soapy shower and I forget about any stings I might have received. That's my solution.

In asthmatics or hyperallergic people, multiple, severe stings may make it difficult to breath. If you run into a cloud of stingers, first get yourself out of the water to a safe position, and then look to see if any other snorkelers nearby are in trouble. If necessary, help get the stung people to a doctor.

The Scrapers

Many books warn against a host of creatures that can scrape you if you drag yourself across them, including coral, barnacles, and others. If we are thinking along those terms, these same books should warn against the dangers of rough handrails, protruding nail heads on docks and any other nefarious scrapers that pose similar dangers.

I cannot imagine what it is like to live with these authors. Do they fear the dire consequences of scraping themselves on a piece of sandpaper while passing through the workroom? Do they fear the hazards of stucco walls? Do they put little corks on the tines of their forks between courses so they will not accidentally abrade themselves? Come on now, people.

As snorkelers, we are committed to touching nothing; thus, we should not be likely to scrape ourselves to death on anything under the water. Just use some common sense and you should be all right.

POPULARLY PESTERED CREATURES

I do not feel kindly toward hotels that dump wild ocean creatures in big glassy tanks so they can be ogled by the ethanol eyes of human guests populating fancy bars. I gnash my teeth at hotels and animal programs that unnaturally crowd ocean creatures together in concrete pools to allow adults and children to paw them without mercy until they wear out and must be replaced. I sharpen my claws at the resorts and dive shops that chum the waters to attract fish, sharks and rays close enough so that their paying customers can intrude into their habitats and disturb their natural feeding and life cycles. It is a definite turn-off for me to see fish, turtles and elasmobranches hanging around like derelicts on the street corner, waiting for handouts, and I am just as chilled by the sight of tourists passing out questionable bait like they were feeding animals at the zoo. I especially want to pounce on the diving books that suggest that you put bait in the water—usually organisms caught nearby and shredded on the spot—to attract carnivorous fish for observation. These baiting techniques do nothing to attract the beautifully colored reef fish that feed on algae and plankton and they could attract unwanted predatory visitors, such as sharks.

Scary Sharks

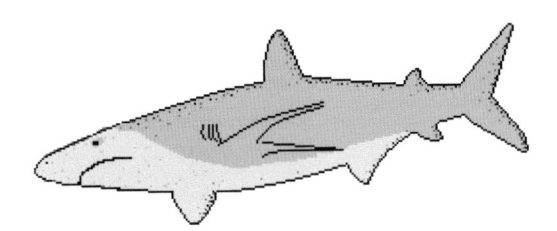

Grey Reef Shark, *Carcharhinus amblyrhynchos*

Sharks appeared about 350-400 million years ago before life had even begun to venture out onto the land. By the time dinosaurs roamed the earth, sharks were already ancient. Sharks belong to the class Chondrichthyes, which means cartilaginous. Sharks, rays and skates are vertebrates whose skeletons are made from flexible cartilage, the same material that makes up your nose.

The World of the Shark

Compared with the pale and frenetic experience of naked apes like us, the world of sharks is spacious, rich and full of sensations. Sharks can detect and follow geological features and living creatures for miles in every direction, and they can even feel the electromagnetic pulse of the earth underneath them, the same as they have ever done. Individual sharks swim the seas around the world and come to know our capacious earth like we know the inside of our punky cars.

These venerables have such a wonderful sense of smell that they can detect one molecule of scent dissolved in a million water molecules. Sharks have such a wonderful sense of hearing that they can hear sounds coming from miles away. Unlike other fish, they still retain an opening into their inner ear, like humans have. They also have the special fish sensory organ called the lateral line that can detect the proximity of other fish by their movement, and they can hear sounds below the range of most human's hearing at 25-50 Hz. Sharks have tiny ampullae on their heads that can detect an electrical signal of half a billionth volt. This means they can detect the presence of other animals in the water by the electric field their bodies generate. Sharks may even be able to navigate by following the minuscule electrical currents produced by the magnetic field of the earth.

Despite what you may have heard, sharks' eyesight is quite good, especially in low light. They have eyelids but they seldom need to blink because the water of the ocean flows over their eyes.

When laymen think of sharks, they often imagine a giant head full of teeth. Sharks' teeth are particularly apparent because they grow from the sharks' faces, not from their jaws. This enables sharks to easily shed and regrow new teeth whenever needed. Sharks' teeth range from thin, needle-like teeth for gripping fish to large, flat teeth adapted for crushing shellfish. Their skin is even protected by a covering of toothlike plates that help guard them from injury.

Most sharks are solitary but others form schools. Sharks may swim thousands of miles every year to return to breeding grounds to mate. Migration patterns in sharks may be even more complex than in birds and many sharks traverse the ocean worldwide. Sharks mate internally and give birth to about a dozen pups. Like humans, shark species' lifespans vary from 40-100 years.

The perception of sharks as dangerous animals has been popularized by fictional works about shark attacks. Absurd shark fantasies have been perpetrated by movies like *The Spy who Loved Me, Live and Let Die, Thunderball, Shark Bait* (an icon of film achievement), *Shark Hunt, Shark Attack I/II/III* and *Spring Break Shark Attack*, as well as countless lurid and biased Discovery, Animal Planet and Natural History Channel television programs that distort the truth about sharks. The author of *Jaws*, Peter Benchley, spent years trying to reverse his smear campaign depicting sharks as dangerous monsters. The spread of fear for profit by the media has caused a genocide of wanton shark slaying, reducing the number of sharks to 10% of their previous natural population.

Sharks have become a shibboleth, almost replacing slithery snakes, slimy bugs and mothers-in-law as objects of cultural fear and loathing. They have become the fictional character of theme parks, including a golf cart-sized head full of rubber teeth lurching toward the Universal Studios tour bus. Sharks have become synonymous with the threat of untamed nature, as scary as our own primitive rage and desire. They represent the unknown, which must ultimately be subjugated to allay our fear of ourselves. Unfortunately, this has nothing to do with the simple, ancient and beautiful animals we call sharks. There is no element of humanity present in the act of hating and killing sharks.

Check with local dive shops and authorities to find out whether sharks are a problem. If anybody tells me that there is a danger of a shark attack somewhere, I simply avoid the place. Although it is frequently said that you are vulnerable to sharks in even shallow water, I feel safe in concluding that you will meet no killer sharks at depths of 3 feet or less. If you should see a shark or something that looks like a shark while snorkeling, just stand up and walk a few feet to the shore or climb on an exposed coral rock. In one or two steps, you should be in a few inches of water where you will be completely safe. The shark will thank you.

Almost none of the advice on what to do if you are confronted by a shark underwater applies to you. I have read terrifying suggestions such as to "face the shark and stare him down," to "hold your ground and not appear afraid," or even to "attack the shark with a club." I have been told, in complete sobriety, that the way to deal with a shark if it comes near you is to hit it on the nose. I find this laughable, and if sharks could laugh, they surely would too. My point is that if a shark comes close enough for me to hit it on the nose, I am in the wrong place.

It's a funny old world. As humans catch, confine and slaughter helpless sharks to provide a few moments of television entertainment, their brethren rove through the sea as they have since the earth was new, dreaming their ancient dreams.

The Redoubtable Rays

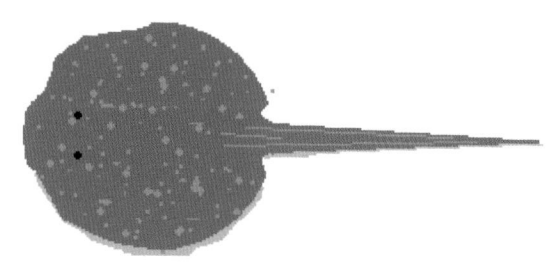

Blue-spotted Stingray, *Taeniura lymma*

Compared with Man Ray, Aldo Rey, and the albedo rays, I find that manta rays are excitingly graceful and beautiful creatures. With wings that allow them to fly through the water, smiling toothless mouths and the ability to leap from the water and bury themselves in the ocean bottom, rays are clearly remarkable characters. Rays do not bite because they have no teeth. Swimming through the ocean, rays direct water into their open mouths, sieving out tiny floating creatures called plankton. Other harmless feeding strategies include burrowing around in the ocean floor to find tiny invertebrates living in the sand. Rays are virtually harmless unless you handle them or step on them. But why would any individual want to handle and frighten a poor a ray? Furthermore, as a good snorkeler endeavors not to stand or walk on the floor of the ocean, the rules of good snorkeling protect both you and the creatures residing on the reef.

Rays are fish with a skeleton of cartilage. They are classified in the order Batoidea, which gives rise to their scientific nickname, batoids. Batoids are most closely related to sharks and young batoids look very much like young sharks. They breathe through gill slits on the underside of the body. Their eyes are located on the top of their heads. They also possess nostrils on the top of their head that they use to breathe water into their gills if they are sitting on the bottom.

Because they are helpless and harmless, rays are a favorite creature for hotels, resorts and diving programs to incarcerate in tanks or herd into crowded cays and lagoons to be handled by doughy tourists for profit. I am sure it makes us feel like the great dominant species to march through a group of toothless rays, but these activities interfere with the animals' natural feeding, social and activity cycles and injure many of the soft creatures in the process. I cannot imagine the horror of a child who has unwittingly participated in this ritual and realizes in later years that he or she has done harm to helpless animals.

Rays are mighty creatures who, as a group, have seen the birth and maturation of our living world. They are not put here for our amusement. My suggestion, as you can imagine, is to respect the rays and to let them live their lives naturally, without human interference, while we observe and enjoy them from afar. In other words, don't pet the rays.

Elusive Eels

Fimbriated Moray Eel, *Gymnothorax fimbriatus*

Eel Larvae

Eels are beautiful creatures. I have seen eels colored bright green, dark brown, and black with brilliant violet pokey dots. Like most eels, morays live in warm waters and coral reefs, where they spend most of their time concealed inside crevices and alcoves, venturing from their holes at night to find the crustaceans and small fish that form their diet.

Although they have big eyes, morays mainly use their acute sense of smell to detect prey at night. Their gills are small and if you see a moray opening and closing her mouth, she is merely breathing, not imagining how you would taste as a people steak between two slices of Wonder bread.

The eel has her own secret, a metamorphosis as mysterious and ethereal as the butterfly unfolding from the chrysalis. An adult eel travels long distances to reach her spawning grounds. After spawning, the eel lays eggs that hatch, not into eels, but into flat, transparent larvae no bigger than 3 inches long. The larvae of some eels travel across the ocean for years until they reach freshwater tributaries, sometimes traveling as many as 30 miles to reach upstream headwaters and ponds. There they metamorphose again into round, pigmented creatures called elvers. Elvers grow over the course of 10-15 years to a length of several feet. Then they travel back to the oceans. Their bodies metamorphose again; their eyes grow and their pigmentation changes. They migrate up to 4,000 miles back across the oceans of the earth to take up residence in their original locations. Eels may live up to 85 years to make all these essential voyages. Compared to the eels' worldwide travels, we crawl through our own human development from childhood through adulthood, never knowing the wonder of the greater seas or the miracle of physical transubstantiation.

Moray eels are harmless enough to be a target for human bullying, poking, prodding and chasing. I find it annoying when groups of people lead night excursions for the purpose of blasting these nocturnal creatures with bright lights just to see their terrified reaction. Is this really necessary or humane?

The scenario goes like this. The leader of a group spots an eel and gets excited. He promptly alerts his buddies who all come rushing up to the poor eel who was minding his own business in the first place. Then a struggle ensues where the humans take turns shining their lights in the helpless eel's face, poking it with their fingers and crowding their facemasks up as close as they can to the poor fellow until he tries to flee. But oh no, that won't do, and all the humans swim in pursuit with scary lights and bubbles while the little eel, now scared out of its mind, tries to find shelter at any cost. Eventually the humans tire of this sport and make way for the next group who chase the eel around some more.

I feel compassionate toward eels because they are so beautiful, so vulnerable and so wise in their vast experience of the world. Please respect the eel by admiring his colors and unique niche in the reef ecostructure from a distance. The god of small creatures thanks you.

The Big, Bad Barracuda

Barracuda, *Sphyraena species*

The barracuda is a 3-6-foot fish with a scary, prognathous jaw. It is common in the Caribbean and in warm ocean waters worldwide. Barracudas belong to the genus *Sphyraena*. Immature barracuda frequently congregate in schools, whereas older, larger barracuda are more likely to be found hunting alone. Barracuda usually hunt by waiting for food fish to come along and grabbing or chasing them at speeds of up to 25 miles per hour.

Barracuda may follow you at a distance across a reef, but the general consensus is that they are harmless unless you try to interfere with them. Barracuda often follow big predatory fish hoping to scavenge the remains of a meal. If visibility is poor or if someone is fishing nearby and there is bait in the water, discretion is the better part of valor and it is best for snorkelers to withdraw.

I remember one day, early in my snorkeling career, when for some reason I chose to swim away from the reef into the open water. After a while, I suddenly noticed that I was not alone. Two barracuda about 4 feet long were keeping pace with me in the water, circling me at a short distance. Both had the annoying habit of clacking their large, powerful lower jaws up and down as they swam, revealing an ample supply of long, pointed teeth. I knew nothing of barracuda at this time but I remembered seeing the same clacking one time when I was stalked by a big cheetah. My response was simply to make a one-eighty turn and swim slowly back to the shallows of the reef where I exited the water and walked safely to the shore.

I was probably in no danger. Barracuda are known for following swimmers around out of curiosity or for some other inscrutable barracuda reason. Were these fish dangerous? Almost assuredly not. Nevertheless, good snorkeling technique requires that you make safety your first priority by making sure that you are never in a situation where anything dangerous might happen. Nowadays, I never see barracuda because I spend all my time snorkeling in the shallow waters where the life is.

The Terrifying Tarpon

Atlantic Tarpon, *Megalops atlanticus*

Our rogues' gallery would not be complete without mentioning the big scary generic fish that lurk in the dark water. For example, one morning I was traveling to a snorkeling site through waters made murky by swirling sand and surf. In the process, I suddenly came upon two tarpon, each over 3 feet long. If I had suddenly bumped into them, would they have investigated me by taking a little nibble of Wes? Probably not, but I simply turned around and took another route. It is easy to be safe while snorkeling if you apply some common sense.

WHY DO WE FRIGHTEN OURSELVES?

In this chapter I have compared real dangers—and how to avoid them—with the media-fueled scare stories that make people hate and fear animals and worry about entering the water. Basically, lurid scare-stories are promoted in order to make money rather than to warn or educate. There are profits to be made from selling scary books, television shows, movies and lectures by irresponsible liars who don't care about the consequences of their actions on our environment. I have frequently seen tour and group leaders using scare tactics to control their groups and make their services seem more desirable. Sometimes intimidators are inadvertently projecting their own insecurity onto their audience. When their listeners are appropriately scared, the intimidators feel justified in their own unreasonable fears. Sometimes the desire to intimidate others results from passive aggression, hostility or plain mean-spiritedness. Whatever the cause, when you are listening to someone talk about the dangers of the ocean and you notice you are feeling anxious or fearful, take a break and do a reality check. Often you will discover that the speaker is trying to frighten you.

CHAPTER 9

SAFETY FIRST

FOR ADULTS, CHILDREN, AND FAMILIES

First, you should realize that although safety is the most important part of snorkeling, the sport is already very safe, especially compared other sports you might try. Snorkeling helps your consciousness stay in the present and because you are focused on what is happening in the surrounding environment, you are more likely to anticipate and avoid potential problems. Using common sense and adopting the mind of a snorkeler will help you avoid almost any dangerous situation, as you will see below. So be informed and aware of safety issues, but do not be worried.

IRRATIONAL DANGERS

Many books and television shows suggest that simply going in the water exposes you to nightmarish dangers such as air embolisms, anoxia, asphyxia, the bends, burst aneurisms, compression toothaches (aerodontalgia), carbon dioxide poisoning, carbon monoxide poisoning, decompression sickness, expansion emphysema, exploded lung, loss of consciousness, high-altitude decompression, hydrocarbon vapor poisoning, nitrogen narcosis, oxygen poisoning, pneumothorax and the so-called rapture of the deep. If you have heard of any of these, then relax and do not worry. These are hazards of SCUBA diving that rarely or never bother snorkelers.

Similarly, problems with broken regulators, emergency ascent, faulty dive computers, fouled hoses, insufficient air, malfunctioning buoyancy controls, torn air hoses and wetsuit tears are confined to those wearing SCUBA diving equipment. Be reassured that by snorkeling, you are avoiding all these woes. The combination of mask, snorkel and flippers is just too simple to cause serious problems.

RELAXATION, ANXIETY, FEAR AND PANIC

The problem I hear most about and which causes the most disturbance before and during snorkeling trips is anxiety. For some, anxiety is an old companion, but for many people, anxiety is associated with new situations significantly different from those of their everyday lives. It is an appropriate reflex to feel apprehension in a strange environment, just as it is natural and safe to be vigilant and alert to anything unexpected. However, when natural vigilance becomes overactive, it can detract from the enjoyment of your trip, or in severe cases, make it impossible for you to do the fun things you planned to do.

The Muscle Relaxation Technique

If you or your children have a problem relaxing, winding down or controlling excitement, try the following exercise. You can find more examples of stress-reduction techniques in my books listed in the Appendix.

Start by lying down. Breathe in and out slowly a few times. Now, slowly breathe in while you contract all the muscles in your toes, feet and legs. Don't hurry. Hold your breath a moment while you keep your muscles tight, then breathe out slowly and relax these muscles. Now, breath in slowly again while you tighten the muscles in your abdomen, shoulders, arms, and fingers. Hold your breath for a moment while keeping these muscles tight, then breathe out slowly and relax them. Now, breathe in slowly while tightening the muscles in your neck and face. Hold this breath for a moment while keeping these muscles tight, then breathe out and relax all your muscles. Now notice your breathing. As you slowly breathe in, imagine you are gathering all the stress in your body. Then, when you breathe out slowly, imagine that you are exhaling all your inner stress along with your breath. Continue this breathing for 30 seconds, a minute, or longer if you like, until you can feel that your body and mind have relaxed. Use the *muscle relaxation technique* to relax before going snorkeling, before or during long airplane trips, and before bedtime to help unwind and get to sleep.

Fear of Flying

Fear of flying is usually the first concern that potential snorkelers face. Sometimes the fear stems from the perceived danger of plane crashes. We have all seen the news media hype horrible calamities from air flight until it seems like horrendous plane crashes happen all the time. However, driving on the highway is more dangerous than flying in an airplane. Just think, how many people do you know who have been involved in an automobile accident? Probably plenty. Now how many people do you know that have been in a plane crash? Not very many. If you are worrying more about crashing in a plane than you do when you are driving on the highway, take an objective look at the reality of the situation and try to adjust your reactions accordingly.

For others, fear of flying is focused on the discomfort of being in a close, cramped space and the perceived difficulty getting out of the plane if they become too agitated. Despite the usual crush on airlines, the problem does not stem from close quarters. After all, you do not panic in the confines of your own bathroom. And surprisingly, most people's feelings of being closed-in dissipate when the plane is off the ground, although the danger of being trapped has increased rather than disappeared.

Unfortunately, logic is usually not sufficient to deal with this type of fear. The first line of defense against this scenario is to do the *muscle relaxation technique* before boarding the plane. Then, bring your music player on the plane and either nap or get lost in your music until the plane is off the ground. If the inside of the cabin is too distracting, you can cover your eyes with a sleep mask—I use my hat.

If your anxiety is too great for these strategies to work, you may wish to see a professional before your trip. Some people have asked their doctors to teach them additional stress reduction exercises or hypnotize them so they can relax before a flight. Your medical doctors may approve using valerian extract. This extract is taken from the root of *Valeriana officianalis,* which has been used forever as a folk medicine for inducing drowsiness.

Fear of the Water

Rarely, I will meet someone in the bar who has been making excuses to stay out of the ocean because they are afraid to tell anyone they are afraid of the water. This is a fairly common fear. I suggest that you begin swimming classes 6-12 months in advance of your trip. Get used to walking, running, swimming and especially treading water in the shallow side of the pool before you graduate to the deeper side. Do the *muscle relaxation technique* before and after entering the water. You will become more comfortable in the water and when you are finally snorkeling and have something exciting to distract your thoughts, you will surely be fine.

Anxiety and Panic Disorders

Some people's anxiety interferes so much with their lives that it takes the form of a disorder. When your mind is preoccupied with excessive worries, especially if it is disturbing your sleep and affecting your work, home life or social life, you may need to be evaluated for a condition known as generalized anxiety disorder. Similar symptoms may be seen in depression and other disorders. These can be controlled with professional help.

Some individuals suffer from overactive adrenaline, called excess adrenergic drive. Physical complaints related to overactive adrenaline include pounding heart, difficulty catching your breath, trembling, nausea, choking, dizziness and excess perspiration. These are also the symptoms seen in panic disorder. These symptoms may show up in specific situations and locations, including flying and snorkeling. Since other medical conditions can also cause similar symptoms, it is a good idea to check with your doctor if you experience them.

One common cause of panic symptoms is rapid breathing (hyperventilation) resulting from excitement or fear. Tingling and numbness around the mouth, fingers or toes is another sign of hyperventilation. Breathing too fast tends to take too much carbon dioxide out of the blood, causing the blood to become more alkaline and the fluid around the brain to become more acidic, triggering panic. The solution is to purposefully breathe slowly or hold your breath at intervals until the episode passes.

After your doctor rules out systemic medical problems, the most important thing to remember is that nobody has ever died from panic disorder. There are self-help books, therapists and doctors that specialize in helping people with panic. If it is a problem for you, turn your panic over to a professional.

DRINKING

I have frequently breakfasted in restaurants where divers and others boasted about getting blind drunk every night. Frankly, this is other people's own business and it may be more exaggeration than excess. Nevertheless, any excursion into an exotic environment like the ocean carries some dangers. When clear logic, perception and coordination stand between you and personal harm, it seems silly to be entering the water either intoxicated or hung over. Moreover, the basic focus of good snorkeling is an awareness of all that is around you and the relationship between you and the life of the reef. Clearly this is not compatible with drinking to excess before a snorkel outing.

I feel a little silly, relating facts that seem quite obvious. However, drinking habits vary much between individuals and it is easy to get into habits of drinking too much or drinking inappropriately. Clearly, alcohol provides some anesthesia from the stress of modern living and pressures that may sometimes be intolerable. At some level, we all would enjoy being popular with friends and successful at partying and carousing with our peers. Alcohol has the well-known ability to grease the wheels of social interaction and make other people's shallow personalities and puerile behavior seem terribly clever. Nevertheless, we are entering the healthful, peaceful environment of the water to provide a respite from the terrestrial world's stress and craziness and we should be able to drop our defensive systems here and try to be our most natural selves.

I have nothing personal against drinking or silliness. In fact, I am well known for offering friends and visitors something to drink and instigating some silly humor. However, you have to be objective about yourself. If you find that you have difficulty putting alcohol aside or it is interfering with other activities in your life, it is time for a reality check. Consider getting some help from a doctor and/or visit an Alcoholics' Anonymous meeting.

MUSCLE CRAMPS

As a child, I was taught to wait 30 minutes after eating a meal before going in the water to avoid getting a cramp. As an adult, I have never been able to substantiate this claim but I have known snorkelers who have experienced cramps of the stomach, arm, leg or other body part while in the water. When I get a leg cramp, I simply stand up, hobble to shore and rub the muscle until the cramp goes away. If I hurt too much to hobble, I turn on my back and propel myself toward the shore with my arms (see Chapter 4).

The only real danger is from a cramp that incapacitates you so that you cannot swim. Instead of sinking like a stone, try one of the floats taught in Chapter 4. On rare occasions when I was incapacitated by a cramp, I just flipped over onto my back and floated until the cramp went away.

Children's cramps are usually more scary than dangerous. Make sure to let children know that if their stomach or their muscles suddenly start to ache, they can just stand up and walk out of the water. If they need help for any reason, they should stand up where they are and wave to the adult who is supervising them. If you are worried that your child might get a cramp, help them do the the *muscle relaxation technique* described above before they go out in the water.

OTHER KNOWN HEALTH PROBLEMS

Make sure you do not have uncontrolled health problems such as asthma, chronic heart failure, chronic obstructive pulmonary disorder, diabetes, emphysema or high blood pressure. If you have not done so already, go to your doctor and get your problems stabilized before you go on your trip. If you have asthma and might need a rescue inhaler while in the water, you can seal one into a zip lock bag. If you have a severe allergy to algae, stings, or a history of anaphylaxis, see if your doctor recommends that you take along a zip lock bag containing an EPI-pen.

NATURAL CONDITIONS

Cold

This may be the most important safety information I can impart to you. If you are in the water and notice that you are getting really cold, head for shore immediately. Come out of the water, sit down on terra firma for a while and then reevaluate whether you should continue your snorkel or head home. I cannot tell you how many times I have noticed I am cold and come out of the water, only to realize in a few minutes that I was fatigued and in no shape to continue snorkeling. Remember, once you warm up and rest up for a moment on the shore, you can always go back into the water but most of the time you will not want to.

If you are supervising children, it is a good idea to require them to come out of the water at 20-minute intervals so you can observe them and see who needs to warm up, rest or quit for the day.

Winds and Currents

If winds or currents come up while you are snorkeling the shallow waters near the shore, you can just stand up and walk onto the land. Since shallow water is the best place for snorkeling anyway, winds and currents should never pose a safety problem. This is why children should never snorkel more than 10 feet from the shore—make sure they stay in water that is shallow enough so that they can stand with their head above the water if they run into any trouble.

However, if you stray too far from the shallow waters of the reef, heavy winds and currents can drive you out to the open ocean. If you are caught in a vicious wind or current and you begin to drift away, point yourself toward the shore and swim like crazy. In this situation, it does not matter where come ashore, as long as you get to dry land. You can worry about how you will get back home or to your car after you are safely out of the water.

If you are snorkeling on a reef far from shore, you are at the mercy of the boat owner that dropped you off there. Before you leave the shore, make sure that any boat owner or agent to whom you trust yourself is reliable and will pick you up at a specific time. Make sure that they are aware of hazardous ocean conditions and that they will come to pick you up forthwith at any sign of trouble.

Tides

Tides are rarely a safety concern for snorkelers. However, in Fiji, for example, if you ignore the timing of the tides, you may find yourself in unexpectedly deep water far from the shore if you are snorkeling on a reef and the tide comes in over your snorkeling site.

What to Do if You Are Drifting

If you are caught in a wind or current and become disoriented or lost, you could look around and suddenly find yourself far from land. If the ocean is calm, point yourself toward shore and employ one of the long-distance, energy-saving swimming strokes described in Chapter 4. If you are too cold and fatigued, the ocean is rough or you can no longer locate land, the next step is to do the *stand and bob float* described in Chapter 4 and wait to be picked up. If this ever happens to you, never give up or lose hope that you will be rescued. The longer you stay afloat, the more likely you are to be spotted and picked up.

Big Waves

If you have been reading this text carefully, you will know that the sport of snorkeling is about peace and harmony, not macho games of who can brave the breakers, power through the pounding surf, or smash through strong seas. What could you hope to see out in rough ocean waves, anyway? The ocean creatures usually retreat from rough seas, and I advise you to do so, also.

The most common danger from waves comes from boats. If a boat does not see the brightly colored tip of your snorkel, it may speed up close to you and slam you with its wake. Depending on the size of the boat, this can disturb your equilibrium or tear off your mask. Staying in shallow water close to the shore and putting bright orange tape on your snorkel can help avoid these situations.

Rain and Storms

When precipitation intrudes or storms threaten, you will see a dramatic downturn in the presence of interesting creatures near the shore. I suspect this is because of decreasing light and temperature. Whatever the explanation, I see nothing to be gained in bucking storms.

If it is a stormy day, just stay out of the water and play Uno until the weather clears. If a storm comes up while you are snorkeling, just pack up and leave the water.

In addition to wind and waves, you may also become a target for lightening if you snorkel in storms. Because the ocean is flat and your head and body stick up slightly from the surface of the water, lightening sparks may discover that you are the highest point to ground. However, good snorkelers do not swim in rain or storms so it is a moot point.

Pregnancy

Pregnant women should have few problems snorkeling. In advanced pregnancy, you are more buoyant and the water will hold you up higher, taking a load off your back that you will welcome. Check with your obstetrician or family doctor before your trip to be sure.

If you are in later stages of pregnancy, you should take extra care to avoid falls and you should enter the water from flat, sandy areas where you will not lose your footing and slip. Anatomy may make it difficult for you to climb ladders into and out of the water, although you can climb sideways in a pinch. In any case, I advise against diving in order to avoid the impact of the water and to prevent landing on invisible objects hiding under the surface.

Knives, Macho Men and Children

For some unknown reason, many snorkelers and divers are obsessed with knives. People make all sorts of lame excuses for buying and carrying knives, like "It will keep me safe from sharks," or "It's in case I get fouled in seaweed," and so forth. The fact is that the opportunity to carry a mean-looking knife where everyone can see it seems cool and macho and it inflates people's egos. Unfortunately, most of the diving knives I have seen (even some expensive ones) are poorly designed and they are made of cheap steel that could not hold an edge well enough to cut anything without skittering around. Such knives will make you a laughingstock around anyone who knows anything about steel. I have known many comrades who have cut themselves playing with their own or someone else's cheesy diving knife. Overall, snorkelers have no use for knives and I do not recommend carrying them.

Worst of all, when these macho knives are shown around, they become attractive to children who want to play like adults but are unaware that they can cut themselves. These children can get seriously hurt. My advice is: 1) don't buy or carry a knife for snorkeling, especially if you have children; 2) don't let other people leave knives out where children can get them; and 3) tell your children they can help you by letting you know whenever they see knives lying about unattended.

SAFETY TIPS FOR CHILDREN AND FAMILIES

- ☑ Drowning can happen in an instant in just a few inches of water. Never leave a young child alone in the water—make sure they are always supervised by an adult you know and trust.

- ☑ Children must never be in water that is over their heads and never more than 10 feet from shore to protect them from being captured by winds or currents.

- ☑ Every child who is going into open water must be able to pass the three snorkeling swimming safety tests described in Chapter 4. Don't let children go in the ocean if they cannot pass these tests.

- ☑ Teach your child the *stand and bob float*, *water boatman stroke*, and *wave rider stroke* from Chapter 4 to use if they become fatigued or become stranded in the open water. This could save their lives.

- ☑ Lead your children in the *muscle relaxation technique* before going into the water. Relaxed muscles are less likely to cramp and relaxed minds exercise better judgment than excited ones.

- ☑ Make sure your children come out of the water at 20-minute intervals so you can observe them and see who needs to rest, warm up or quit for the day.

- ☑ Ask older children and teens to read this book to inform themselves about safety issues before entering the water.

CHAPTER 10
SNORKEL WITH WES
AN EVERYDAY SNORKELING ADVENTURE

Let's go on a snorkel excursion together, where you can see everything you know about snorkeling put into practice.

It's a nice new day and I've had plenty of high protein food for breakfast, such as Gouda cheese, eggs, and Dutch or Swedish ham. I eat fruit in the form of fresh melon, papaya, guava and pineapple, adding fruit juice, water or espresso. I don't worry about reducing salt intake because I will be exercising all day and the ocean water acts like a diuretic. A little extra salt helps me hold on to my body fluid.

I'm up early but I wait until the sun has warmed the reef before I head for the water. In the meantime, I gather my gear together.

Today my fins are a pair of medium priced, strap-on models that I chose because they are very flexible and they fit well. Long ago, I glued the twinky strap buckles shut and adjusted the straps to fit perfectly and I have not changed them since. After I last used these fins, I washed them in fresh, warm, soapy water and dried them in the sun. Now they are clean and ready to go. I pull out a small duffel bag and stuff them inside. Like all my equipment, my fins and duffel bag are labeled with my name and telephone number drawn in large letters with a black marker.

My mask is a very-low-volume model with a black silicone skirt and neon green trim. The lenses are color-corrected pink polycarbonate for better visibility. Years ago, I consulted with a friendly optometrist and had the lenses ground so they focus optimally at 3-6 feet, a common viewing distance on the reef. By the way, I replaced the rubber strap on the mask with a non-stretchy Velcro strap that I adjusted so the mask fits perfectly. Like the fin straps, I haven't changed the adjustment of the mask since. The back of the strap is a broad, closed-cell foam pad that distributes the pull of the mask across the back of my head and doesn't pull my hair.

After I last used this mask, I washed it in warm, soapy water and left it to dry on the dish drainer by the sink. Last night I rubbed Ocean View anti-fog solution over the entire inside of the mask and sat it back in the dish drainer overnight. Now I just give the mask a light rinse under the faucet and it's ready.

The snorkel I will use today is already connected to the right side of the mask strap with a bit of neoprene. My snorkel is an inexpensive model with a purge valve that flushes out any drops of ocean spray that may find their way down the tube. The tube is connected to the mouthpiece with a flexible vinyl hose, which automatically adjusts to the angle of my mouth. I replaced the original, ill-fitting rubber mouthpiece with a silicone SCUBA-divers' bite-strip that I purchased for $1.00 at a dive shop and force fit onto the snorkel. Unless I have to service either snorkel or mask, I keep them attached permanently. I grab the mask and connected snorkel, and stick them inside a big polyethylene bag so the mask will not be scratched. Then I pop the works into the duffel bag.

Today I will cover my skin for warmth and for protection from sun, stings and scrapes. I consider a long-sleeved nylon shirt and pants but I reject them in favor of a full-body nylon/Lycra dive skin colored light blue with a grey wavy pattern to match the ocean. It takes a little effort to pull the light suit over my body because it fits tightly, but it will keep me warm, smooth my passage through the water and protect my own skin from fire coral and jellyfish stings. I pull up the zipper in front.

While I wait for the sunscreen to dry, I find a place to sit down and attend to my feet. I pick out a pair of clean, dry, nylon bootie socks and slip them over my feet. These particular socks are pink nylon tubes—it was the only color they had. They will keep my feet warm and help my neoprene booties slide on and off with ease. Bootie socks also make my booties and fins fit better and feel more comfortable.

My strap-on fins wouldn't fit perfectly without a pair of close-fitting neoprene booties underneath. The ones I choose today are ankle-high black neoprene booties that close with a nylon side zipper. I chose this pair today because they have a sturdy rubber sole like a pair of tennis shoes that will help me walk to the area where I will be snorkeling today. If I have to leave the water at some distance from my entrance point, I know I can walk back without getting blisters or abrading my feet. The last time I used these booties, I washed them in warm, soapy water, rinsed them and poured in a little Listerine mouthwash before setting them in the sun to dry. Now they are clean, dry and odor-free. I slip the booties on easily over my slick bootie socks and I pull up the zippers.

Now I grab my tube of SPF 70 sunscreen and go to work. I rub it on the back of my neck, my ears and the backs of my hands—the only places not covered by my mask and dive skin. Then I rinse off my palms and rub them with a small towel. The towel goes in my duffle bag and I zip it up. Now, I grab my duffel bag and take a leisurely stroll down to the nearby dock.

You may wonder why I am going to a public dock instead of getting in my four-wheel-drive vehicle and driving out to some special location that nobody knows about but me. Simply stated, there's no need to. Even when the ocean is filled with surface swimmers and SCUBA divers, there are always shallow, undisturbed areas near the shore where the wildlife is abundant. Even in this familiar area, I can spend all day seeing new things on the reef and I can come back day after day and still see more. Also, the less time I spend traveling, the more time I'll have for snorkeling. And I'd rather travel on my heels than on wheels that need to be fed with polluting fossil fuel. So everybody benefits from my short walk to the dock.

At the dock, I take out my flippers, mask and snorkel, and weigh down the empty duffel bag with a rock so it won't blow away. Even if it does, the name and number I wrote on it will help it come back to me. I put my mask strap over my head and leave it hanging around my neck with the snorkel dangling from the mask strap. I insert my left hand through the straps of both fins, leaving them dangling from my wrist. Then, with both hands free, I climb down the ladder into the water. It is always a shock when the cold water hits my torso but the dive skin buffers the transition and it passes in a moment.

Once in the ocean, I paddle away from the dock, where I will be free from swimmers, divers and boat traffic. There, I float in the water like I was sitting in an easy chair, pulling up my mask and pulling my fins on over my booties. Meanwhile, I watch a 300 lb. man hold onto his nose and dive heavily off the dock in a crouching position like he was in a Sea Hunt movie. His plunge throws up cascades of seawater and scatters both children and fish. There's always a clown in the bunch. After my fins are attached, I make a quick 360-degree turn in the water to spot the locations of divers, boats, nets and other obstacles. I set the dot on my rotating watch dial to the minute hand. Then I put the snorkel in my mouth, I put my face into the water and I begin swimming.

First, I'll check under the dock. As I expect, I see a big tarpon called Charlie lurking near the bottom. There are a few blue tang, pale in the dimness under the dock, treading water so they can stay at the same distance from and orientation to each other. An 8-foot cloud of schooling silversides are congregated near the surface, feeding. Swimming under the dock, I discover a 3-inch red and white banded shrimp, with a tangle of long segmented legs and antennae, clinging to the wooden pilings. I look but don't touch for a few minutes before swimming out from under the dock.

I move in close to the shore where the water is 3-5 feet deep. It's warm and comfortable for me as a snorkeler, and that's where everything interesting lives. At this depth, a SCUBA diver in a wetsuit and a giant tank strapped to his back could only flounder and his bubbles and noise would chase all the fish into hiding. This is a snorkeling zone.

I power myself with my arms, sliding through the water like a fish. I stop my arm strokes for a moment and squeeze my fins together once to speed my passage, until I'm floating in 4 feet of water that is warmer and clearer than near the dock. Below me are rocks covered with yellow and fiery orange coral; pastel blue and violet sponges; and purple, neon pink and electric blue anemones. Nearby are the remains of four giant concrete pylons torn from a former dock long ago. Over the years, these pylons have been colonized and now look just like the natural rocks.

Floating in the water, I am beyond the reach of the human world. I can do what I want, and in this case, I choose to do nothing. I stop all motion and lay flat on the surface with my arms and legs spread wide and my fin tips anchoring me in the water. I feel so warm and comfortable I could easily fall asleep. Instead of sleeping, I start observing. Below me, I spot about six damselfish about one-half-inch long, colored a brilliant iridescent blue interlaced with eye-popping sky-blue spots from tip to tail. They are flitting about inside the spikes of a pincushion urchin feeding on barely visible macroscopic creatures swimming around the urchin's spines. Somewhere nearby, dark-colored adult damselfish with light yellow tails are guarding territory, tending gardens of algae, and protecting their eggs. The juveniles I am watching differ from adults in location, appearance, food choice and behavior, so they never compete with one other.

Next to the urchin are several cone-shaped, snaily gastropods called *Corus*. They are pink and sit firmly on the rock. If they are moving at all, they are slow as, well, snails. Their crusty pink and lime green color would set them apart in our drab terrestrial world but *Corus* blend in so well with the hues of the reef that they are barely visible.

A passing wave comes makes the spines of the pincushion urchin tinkle, reminding me that they are not just rocks with spines but they are a member of the ancient class of echinoderms. Like starfish, the legless urchins are designed in a radial pattern with a star motif clearly visible inside their bodies. They move on soft tubular feet operated by water under pressure, like hydraulics. In the center is a mouth with five teeth that scrubs algae from the rocks on which they sit.

Now the current is moving me away. If I wanted, I could just flip the corner tip of my fin and stay in position, but I'd rather drift. Slowly another rock covered with 2-10-inch patches of yellow reticulated brain coral and antler-like yellow-orange fire coral appears below me. I remember grabbing onto an underwater ladder last year and getting a nasty sting from a bit of fire coral the size of my thumbnail. However, I never come close to touching anything on the reef, so thoughts of fire coral's stings or spiny urchins' prickles are far from my mind.

I hear something that resembles a man chewing a mouthful of iceberg lettuce. It is a stoplight parrotfish, chewing algae from the rocks for his dinner. I am within touching distance of the parrotfish and he is watchful for a minute, but as he sees that I do not move, he goes about his business like I was invisible. This fish would stand out at Mardi Gras. His head is blue with teal stripes, circled with hot pink at the gill covers. His fins are striped electric blue, his body scaled in iridescent blue and green. His tail is banded into bright teal, jade and blue. On his head and tail are brilliant dots of lemon yellow, like bits of custard. This is the stoplight parrotfish's final adult color. A younger adult is swimming below him, and although they are identical in shape, the two fish could not appear more different. The younger adult's body is a checkerboard of iridescent maroon and mother of pearl, whereas his belly and lower fins are colored bright red. As they grind their mouthfuls of coral rocks to release the algae, cascades of white sand pour out in a cloud from their gill slits and settle with similar granules on the ocean floor. Another large parrotfish, the rainbow, comes into view as I turn my head. The rainbow parrotfish also has an iridescent green tail; however, his lips are bright robins' egg blue and his head is international orange. What a work of art!

I flip the tip of my flip and glide 5 feet forward. Now my arms are behind my back, resting on my posterior, with the thumb of one hand held in the palm of the other. This pose streamlines my body so that I glide smoothly through the water and it keeps my upper appendages out of sight so they don't dangle down and scare the fish. As I float up to another cluster of coral, I spread my legs and let the tips of my flips drop down, stopping me and stabilizing my position in the water.

We think of coral as a rock, but it is really a giant apartment house for small creatures called anthozoan polyps. Each polyp stays in its shell and communicates with the outside world by tiny tentacles stuck out of the door. These tentacles sieve passing food like a net.

I can see fist-sized patches of red, orange and clashy purple that look like a painter was cleaning his brushes on the rocks and coral below me. These are another type of ancient invertebrate called bryozoans who live in colonies with specialized classes for feeding, reproduction and defense. Next to them are the large patches of fire-engine red, orange and yellow encrusting sponges. In a rock crevice, I see a 5-inch bunch of translucent lime green tubes gracefully waving in the water. Next to them is a similar corsage of white tubes capped by bulbar purple heads. Both of these are sea anemones. Their relatives, the jellyfish, can sometimes be seen swimming through the water.

Another kick and I move on a few feet, taking the opportunity to relax and feel the warmth of the sun on my covered back. The waves wash me back and forth in a gentle massage. I feel no pressure, no time and no gravity. I am floating in another world, at peace within the geologic womb of life, sharing this world in harmony with all the diverse ocean creatures. No matter how hard I tried, I could never find more beauty or excitement than floating here in the sunny water surrounded by riotous color and motion. If I ache for the excitement of exploring new realms, all I have to do is swim a little farther and look a little closer. There is a lifetime of mystery to be found in each square foot of reef below me.

A school of 20 blue tang glide alongside me; their saucer-sized bodies swim in unison as they dart in and about the rocks. All are the same size, but some are midnight blue, others electric blue and a few are pastel baby blue or white. Inside the school, a Spanish hogfish with an electric purple body and golden belly swims side-by- side with the tang, unnoticed by them. A foot from the school, half a dozen 5-inch, gold and black-striped sergeant majors investigate the rocks together. At mating time, the males will become dusky blue, build circular nests and attract females by swimming in circles. When a female lays her eggs in the nest, the male sergeant major will then guard them until they hatch.

A single bluehead wrasse swims by. He is a cigar-shaped fish with a deep blue head and an iridescent green tail separated by broad vertical stripes of black, white and black. Perhaps he's looking for a tiny yellow female with whom to mate. If a sexually mature female cannot find a mate, she simply changes color, becomes a male and mates with another female.

Now I see a little chocolate-brown head with a broad red grin poking out from a hole in the rock below. And there is another. And another. I'm seeing a host of 3-inch, red-lipped blennies. The bright red lines drawn across their faces make these blennies look decidedly like circus clowns. As I look across the rock, I now see many blennies resting on their red-tipped fins and surveying their small territories. At some point, females will lay their eggs inside the males' holes, leaving the males to guard and care for the eggs and baby hatchlings. For now, the red-lipped blennies are content to dart from their holes to chase away intruders. When a cloud suddenly passes overhead, all the little chocolate-brown heads disappear down their holes.

Just as the blennies disappear, I catch another glimpse of movement. Underneath a head of brain coral, I see another head peering out. It belongs to a 5-inch brown eel with sky blue spots who is waiting until night to show herself. Under the adjoining coral head, I see a black bar soldier fish hiding. With his bright, rosy golden color and enormous eyes, this 6-inch swimmer looks like a Brobnagonian goldfish transposed from his tank in the pet store. The edges of his gill covers are stark black in contrast with his reddish golden body, making up the vertical black bar for which he is named.

After lying motionless for several minutes, a tiny, round fan in the shape of a feather duster unfurls on the top of the coral. As I continue to wait, other fans come popping out of the coral, producing a bouquet of white, orange, pink and yellow fans. Never in a million years could we guess that these beautiful structures are food-catching nets attached to the heads of worms hidden inside the rocks. Again, with the slightest disturbance, the bouquets suddenly vanish.

I remain motionless and two 1-inch yellow Christmas trees appear next to the feather dusters on the same coral head. As I look around, I realize that 10 or 20 more pairs are now visible. These delicate yellow Christmas tree fronds, always seen in pairs, are also food-catching nets attached to the head of secluded worms living beneath the rock surface. Plankton that collide with the fronds are swept downward into the Christmas tree worm's mouths.

Not all fish look fishlike. When I turn slightly to the side, I see a black pea with white polka dots wobbling by on her pectoral fins. "What a funny little piece of baggage," I think, as this is the juvenile smooth trunkfish. Underneath her swims an adult trunkfish of the same species. He has a flat belly, peaked back and a body that looks like a 6-inch pyramid. He swims leisurely, pausing at intervals to poke at the sand with his snout-like mouth. His body is dark with white spots, and next to him, we can see another adult trunkfish, identical except for a magnificent iridescent purple body. A little higher in the water rides a shiny vertical bar about 1 foot long and less than 1 inch in diameter. This is the trumpet fish, a master at camouflage and color change. He may be seen, or perhaps I should say unseen, in colors of reddish-brown, blue or bright yellow.

A cloud of bottom sand belies the position of a yellow goatfish. She is 6-8 inches of silver with a bifurcated yellow tail and a bright lemon stripe stretching from tail to eye. On the front of her mouth, a pair of whiskers called barbels help her shovel aside the sandy ocean floor, looking for tasty morsels buried there. Another silvery fish looks on at the goatfish's side, hoping to catch any edible creatures that she leaves behind. Just above them, a school of 20 yellow goatfish swims in unison, flashing yellow and silver against the ocean blue.

I finally find the bathing beauty of the reef. A 3-inch cluster of pink, yellow and white blossoms in a floral arrangement is slowly crawling across the ocean bottom. Occasionally the waves brush the blossoms aside and we can see the lime green underside of *Elysia*, the lettuce sea slug.

Now I am close to the shore, where the coral rock rises like a straight wall. Along the wall, the black needles of our friends the long-spined sea urchins present their prickly pincushions. Next to them are little 5-inch blobs of one-half-inch wide, bright orange cups. These are called, reasonably enough, orange cup coral. As the light decreases at day's ends, bright fronds will appear from the cups to sieve the sea for tiny plankton. Between the black urchins and orange cups I see tiny, 2-inch nimble spray crabs, colored black with neon orange knees and neon green stripes across the front of their heads. For a moment, they mill around, warily scuttling sideways across the wall. As they settle down, we can see their little legs whirling in front of their tiny mouths, gathering in the tiny sea creatures of the reef. As my mask breaks the surface of the water, I see their brethren, the blotched swimming crabs, who spend their days above the waterline. These 2-6-inch crabs pick their way sideways across the coral, watching me intently with their bright eyes turning on little stalks. The contrast of their quiet purple, maroon and brown color scheme with the riotous colors beneath the waves is startling. Along the same wall above the water, 3- and 4-inch chitons lay pressed flat into depressions in the wall waiting as they have done since the earth was young. As if to prove they are not fossils, a particularly big chiton moves ever so slightly, nestling closer to the rocky wall. A curious tourist sees me observing and calls down in a friendly voice, "What's that thing you got there?"

"A chiton," I reply. Finished with my snorkeling, I remove fins and climb out of the water.

After the Snorkeling's Over

I hope you were amazed and encouraged at my report of just a few of the things you could see any day in a 20-minute drift down the reef. Here is what I do after every snorkeling outing.

First, I shake off my sandy booties and carry them, along with my fins, mask and snorkel, straight back to the shower. There I turn on the warm water and get in without taking off my nylon dive skin. I grab a bar of mild soap and stand under the water, soaping and rinsing everything. After my mask, snorkel, booties and fins are clean, they go into the nearby sink to drain. I run a little more warm water on my dive skin and take it and my bootie socks off under the shower spray. These join my other equipment in the sink.

Now there is a naked man in the shower. I wash his hair, face and body with hot water and liberal squirts of Betadine scrub soap. It is available in most drug stores or it can be ordered over the Internet. This iodine-based, non-staining soap has antibacterial and antifungal properties. If you've sustained any cuts or scrapes during your snorkel, it is the perfect disinfectant.

After my shower, I drop off my mask in the kitchen sink, hang up my dive skin and arrange my socks and fins outside in the sun to dry. I shake all the water from my booties and pour a half-capful of Listerine into each, shake it around and pour it out. This procedure keeps evil denizens from growing in the neoprene. If the booties smell like dead feet, I put two sprays of Bactine down each one instead of the mouthwash. Then the booties go outside in the sun next to the socks and fins.

Now I check my body for any scrapes, cuts or stings. I usually have a few abrasions, even if they just occurred from stumbling to or from a snorkeling site. These get the Bactine treatment. Then I spray Bactine between my toes to prevent any fungus infection there.

When my dive skin, socks, fins and booties are accounted for, I go back to the kitchen and wash my mask inside and out with warm, sudsy water and mild detergent. When it dries, the inside of each lens gets a squirt of Ocean View Defog, which I spread all over the lenses and the entire interior surface of the mask with my fingers. Then I put the mask aside and let everything dry until my next snorkel. Yes, yes, I know this is not what the directions say to do, but this approach works best in all my tests. Just remember to rinse out your mask before you go in the water.

Finally, I drink some water and take a 20-minute nap.

THE THREE COMMANDMENTS OF SNORKELING RESPONSIBILITY

These are the basic rules for responsible behavior that you need to think about and accept *before* entering the world of water-dwelling creatures.

I. "Accept the Law of Reciprocity"

Cause and effect works two ways. When you refuse to touch surrounding coral, you protect the coral creatures and you avoid scraping yourself. When you refuse to step on the bottom, you avoid injuring the urchins and rays living there and they do not puncture you. By protecting the integrity of snorkeling sites, you ensure that they will be attractive for others, and you will enjoy them more when you return. When you help other creatures, you help yourself as well.

II. "The Reef is Not a Toy"

Don't be infantile and try to play with the reef or its inhabitants. Don't poke them to see what they will do or scare them to see them run away. The creatures are not there for your amusement. They are living their own lives. Remember that you are just a guest who has no business interfering in the lives of others. Stay in the background where you belong.

III. "Act Like a Responsible Adult"

Exercise empathy and compassion at all times. Empathy is the capacity to put yourself in another's place. Compassion is the capacity to feel for another. Be mature, responsible, empathic and compassionate in your dealings with every individual from the smallest of aquatic creatures to the other humans you will encounter while snorkeling. Be an ambassador for the snorkeling sport.

CHAPTER 11
HOW TO PACK FOR A SNORKELING TRIP

Knowing what I do now, I would have paid a pretty price for a comprehensive packing list to use on my first snorkeling trips. Now, after compiling definitive lists for myself and others for over 20 years, I am happy to share my packing lists with you.

There are really two reasons you need packing lists. The first is so that you do not forget to pack the things that you will need. The other reason you need packing lists is to anticipate the things that you will need to handle critical situations that haven't come up yet. That's where my experience comes in handy. In addition, the right packing list can help you save time, keep you from arriving with too much or not enough stuff and help you coordinate your packing with spouses, friends, children and other essential members of your party.

Feel free to remove these pages from your book to take shopping or to use while packing. This first, most important list contains all the things you should take or consider taking on every trip.

ESSENTIAL ITEMS FOR A ONE-WEEK TRIP

Books, Periodicals, Pencils and Paper

Buy and bring animal picture identification guides for fish, marine invertebrates, birds, reptiles, local mammals and whatever you want to understand better in your new environment. You can read these on the plane to help prepare you for your trip. I carry a complete set of hardbound guides by P. Humann and N. DeLoach everywhere I go. See the Appendix.

If you bring inexpensive paperback novels for entertainment, you can recycle by leaving them at your destination for other people to read when you leave. I also tuck in magazines that I have not yet got around to reading. Budding authors and artists should bring pens, pencils and a notebook for making sketches, recording nature observations and writing rough drafts of their own snorkeling books.

I discourage you from bringing Kant, Niche, Dostoyevsky, Kafka or books about airplane crashes, toxic oil spills or shark attacks. For Pete's sake, don't bring work-related material to catch up on during your vacation. Instead, pack some fun novels that will make you smile at the end of the day when you are too tired to do anything else.

Cell Phone

If you bring your telephone, it's a good idea to buy some local minutes or just pick up a disposable local telephone. Then look up and write on or program the numbers of the local emergency room and police department. You'll be glad they are there if you need them.

Listerine

Named after Joseph Lister, the pioneer of sterile surgery, Listerine is a mouthwash of many uses. In addition to dental hygiene, you can use it as a disinfectant for cuts and scrapes. Give the inside of your neoprene booties a rinse of Listerine and you can prevent the foot fungus that gives rise to stinky boot syndrome and the dreaded dead foot disease. I also bring along a disinfecting povidone iodine soap that I use to wash myself and my gear in the shower after every snorkel outing.

Nasal Spray

If you have sinus problems or ear difficulties, or in case your ears do not clear at high altitude, bring along some 12-hour nasal decongestant spray. This stuff can save your snorkeling trip if you start to get a cold or allergy while snorkeling. Any nasal spray with oxymetazoline as the only active ingredient will do.

Rain Clothes

Bring something to deal with sudden, brief or prolonged showers, especially if traveling in Florida or the Caribbean. Keep it simple; a yellow rain slicker or a waterproof nylon poncho in a plastic pocket will serve you well. Because it does rain in paradise.

Shaving

Forget about bringing electric razors. I know they can hold a charge for days and they are supposed to run on all kinds of bizarre foreign voltages but they are heavy, bulky to pack, and when you get to your destination, there is always something to go wrong. I go to the drug store and buy the fanciest disposable razors they have and I don't take them out of their package until I get to my destination. They always work fine for me.

Shoes

Only take tried and true shoes that have been well broken in. Unplanned walks and long exposure to high humidity and seawater can raise unexpected blisters and cause painful feet at the worst moments. Instead of those toney new togs you spotted at the mall or in the catalog, bring well-worn sandals, friendly flats or tennies that can get wet and dry quickly. Bring an extra pair of slippers or flip-flops to lounge around in and to wear when your other shoes are drying out.

Sunblock

Get the kind that blocks UVA and UVB rays, called "broad spectrum." I try to find one with an SPF value of 70 or more.

Sunglasses

Make sure you have UV blocking, neutral grey, polycarbonate-lensed sunglasses. You can find industrial safety glasses in a wealth of attractive styles and colors that are so inexpensive you may want to buy several to have a backup. See the Appendix.

Sun Shades

Bring a wide-brimmed hat. Panama hats, Mexican sombreros and other ventilated hats can help you stay cool in the sun, and they can protect you from harmful, carcinogenic solar radiation. I particularly like the Tilley hat (see the Appendix). Take one or more bandanas in bright, cheerful colors for neck protection.

Toiletries

Take small sample sizes of soap, shampoo and toothpaste that you obtain at large chain drug stores. Then, at the end of the trip, you just throw them away and you don't have to carry back partially empty bottles. The luggage inspectors will love you for this.

Urban Defense Tools

Don't forget to bring nail clippers, nail files, emery boards, tweezers and any other grooming tools you use on a regular basis. Sometimes these little necessities are hard to find on islands or in isolated locations.

Dental Hygiene

OK. You *will* remember to bring your toothpaste and toothbrush without my reminders. But don't forget the dental tape or floss.

Natural Medicine Chest

Go out and find a bottle of Underberg or Angostura bitters. A tablespoon of either of these can work wonders for an upset stomach. If you have trouble sleeping, consider getting a bottle of valerian extract from the health food store. It is an herbal preparation that has been used for inducing sleep back as far as the Babylonians. At least that is what the clay tablets say.

Unnatural Medicine Chest

To reduce inflammation and speed the healing of sunburns and minor sprains and strains, bring some plain aspirin or ibuprofen. Tylenol can relieve headaches but it has little anti-inflammatory efficacy. Also, ask your local physician to recommend and prescribe a general antibiotic to treat travelers' grippe. Women should remember that sulfa drugs—often prescribed for urinary tract infections—tetracyclines, clarithromycin and ciprofloxacin, are probably not safe to use if you are pregnant. Consult your doctor.

Attitude

Don't lose sight of the fact that these trips are for fun. They are not meant to generate worries, induce preparation frenzy or trigger anticipatory anxiety. When in doubt, leave it at home. Odds are that you won't need it anyway. If you forget to bring something, that's what money is for. My professor's aunt used to say, "When possible, pack half as much stuff and bring twice as much money."

PACKING LISTS FOR EVERY BUDGET AND LEVEL OF EXPERTISE

The Neophyte's List of Recommended Snorkeling Gear

- ☑ The best-fitting mask you can find, borrow or buy cheaply
- ☑ Diluted dishwashing detergent for defog solution
- ☑ Flexible pull-on fins
- ☑ Any snorkel that doesn't leak
- ☑ Close-fitting, long-sleeved tee shirts for sun protection and cold-water warmth
- ☑ Thin pants or jeans for sun protection and cold-water warmth
- ☑ Canvas tennis shoes
- ☑ Any watch that is waterproof to 10 feet or more

The Intermediate Snorkeler's List of Recommended Snorkeling Gear

- ☑ The best-fitting mask you can find. Pick one with a wide field of view and low volume.
- ☑ Sea Vision defog solution
- ☑ Dive booties
- ☑ Flexible strap-on fins
- ☑ Any snorkel with a purge valve
- ☑ Nylon dive skin, either separate top and pants or a full-body suit, for protection from cold, sun, and fire coral
- ☑ Povidone iodine soap (Betadine) for washing yourself and your gear
- ☑ Any watch waterproof to 20 feet with a rotating bezel to measure how long you have been in the water

The Expert's List of Recommended Snorkeling Gear

- ☑ A great-fitting mask, with a wide field of view and low volume that is ground to your eyeglasses prescription. If you have two masks, you can let one dry with defog solution while you use the other.
- ☑ Neoprene mask replacement strap
- ☑ Sea Vision defog solution
- ☑ Any snorkel with a purge valve
- ☑ Dive socks
- ☑ Dive booties. If you bring two pairs of booties, you can let one pair dry while you use the other pair.
- ☑ Flexible strap-on fins, tuned for top performance. If you bring another pair of pull-on fins, you can use these for casual snorkel outings while your main pair of fins, booties and dive socks dry out.
- ☑ Nylon dive skin for protection from cold, sun, and fire coral. If you've invested this much of your time and money in this sport already, you might as well buy one with a cool pattern on it. I always take at least two dive skins so I will not have to put on a wet one—ugh!
- ☑ Povidone iodine soap (Betadine) for washing yourself and your gear
- ☑ Waterproof dive watch with a rotating bezel to measure how long you have been in the water

- ☑ Tiny binoculars for watching birds, iguanas and other snorkelers
- ☑ Big, tough luggage to pack things that the airlines cannot destroy. I use waterproof luggage made by the Pelican Company (see the Appendix). It's a little heavier than some but it is wicked waterproof and guaranteed against breakage from any cause except small children.

FIRST AID KIT

It is prudent to carry along a more complete first aid kit to be prepared for minor problems. You will have no fun driving all over the island on Sunday morning looking for band-aids, triple antibiotic ointment or a finger cot. If you don't have time to put your own together, you can spend more money and buy one from LLC, in the Appendix. If you collect your own first aid items, you can find or buy a waterproof box to put them in. I just keep mine in a polyethylene Ziploc bag.

Band Aids

Everybody always needs these, the bigger the better. Those tiny little strips and dots are great for kids but only the big ones are really functional. On the other hand, if can find large bandages printed with stars and stripes that you want to use, go crazy. Large strips can always be cut down if you need smaller ones.

Bactine

Just as it did when you were a kid, Bactine helps kill germs and relieve the pain of minor cuts, scrapes, mosquito bites and mild sunburn. As an adult, you will find that a few sprays can protect you from foot fungus and keep your booties from smelling. Use it to sterilize your scissors if you are cutting sterile gauze.

Povidone Iodine Soap (Betadine)

I use this for everything, but it is essential if you have a deep scrape or cut. These need to be cleaned and scrubbed with a nailbrush loaded with antiseptic soap. No kidding, it hurts like the Dickens but it has to be done. The alternative is to go to an emergency room and pay to have a doctor scrub it for you. This is the best way to remove foreign matter caught under your skin. If you do not remove it, it will heal in there and/or cause an awful infection.

Sunburn and Sting Relief

Get a tube of pure aloe gel and/or a bottle of Solarcaine. Both seem to work equally well, but I prefer the aloe gel. Once on a research trip, I was stung across my back and shoulders by hundreds of thousands of ants. These two products kept me from going batty during the 3-month healing process.

Topical Wound Dressing

A tube of triple antibiotic ointment, available at the drug store, is usually satisfactory. My true favorite is a polymer-based lotion called Animax, which combines several anti-infectious agents plus a low dose of steroids. However, it is a veterinary product that is not licensed for human use and it must be obtained over the Internet or from a veterinarian.

Wound Closures

These are available under the heading of butterfly bandages. Butterfly bandages are handy to close up a cut so that it heals better or to hold a gash together until you get to the doctor to have it stitched. I have closed many wounds with butterfly bandages that would otherwise have had to be sutured.

Zinc Oxide Crème

Zinc oxide crème is magical. I was introduced to its use by a man who had studied German folk medicine in the 1930s. It is called an emollient but I really do not know how it works. I have seen it annihilate rashes, itches and skin problems of many years' duration. In a pinch, it will serve as a waterproof sun block.

Antihistamine

If you run into an allergy on your trip, this could come in handy. However, if someone in your party has an anaphylactic reaction to a bite, sting or food allergy, the right antihistamine could be life-saving on the way to the hospital for an adrenaline injection. I prefer capsules containing diphenhydramine that are available at the drug store. Remember that any severe allergy reaction where it becomes difficult to breathe is an obligatory ticket to the emergency room.

Eye Drops

Get the moisturizing ones with glycerin to wash out your eyes if sand, dust or chlorine gets into them.

Finger Cot

I have a funny story about a finger cot. When you see what they look like, you will understand why. Finger cots are little rubber sleeves that cover your finger to keep water away from a minor wound. If you have a dressing on your finger that you want to keep dry, slip on a finger cot and jump in the water.

Gauze, Tape and Scissors

I carry three 3 x 3-inch square gauze pads in sterile paper envelopes. You will have to buy a box of these and take out three. Use them with tape for bandaging a burn or wound. If you need smaller ones, just cut them with your scissors. A pair of blunt-tipped surgical scissors with 3-inch blades is best. The next best choice is manicure scissors from the dime store. Disinfect them with Bactine, Betadine or vodka.

CARIBBEAN COOKING KIT

If you are a big fan of Caribbean tropical fruits like I am, it may be worth your while to carry some specialized cooking and food preparation tools. Here are the ones I take with me.

Fruit Peeler

A sharp, ceramic fruit peeler works great on guavas and papayas. Peel the fruit, cut it up and serve with lime and chili pepper, Guadalajara style.

Pineapple Slicer

There is nothing like fresh tropical pineapple. You will find that a pineapple slicer makes short work of thorny ripe pineapple. You just lop off the top and bottom and twist the pineapple slicer through the fruit. I can core and slice a big, fat tropical pineapple in 30 seconds with one of these babies. Yummy.

Mango Slicer

The young man at my local tropical fruit stand chops up mangos in short order, but I cannot seem to get the hang of it, myself. It's that strange, giant, sticky seed in the middle. If you cut too close to it, your knife gets stuck, you cut off fibrous pieces of seed stuff and you are likely to slip on the sticky thing and cut your hand. If you slice too far away from the seed, you miss the sweet meat of the fruit. Finally, I found a mango slicer. Just align it with the top of the fruit, push it down and it cuts close around that seed in the middle, leaving loads of just pure fruit. Essential for hard-core mango lovers like me.

CHAPTER 12
SNORKELING SEMINAR:
ANSWERS TO YOUR SNORKELING QUESTIONS

Q: **What's the most important skill I can develop to improve my snorkeling experience?**

A: Cultivate the ability to stay perfectly still in the water with your complete attention on just one spot. Sometimes I will stay motionless for 15 minutes without taking my eyes off a fish or a dark hole, waiting for its inhabitant to come out. Try this. Look at the "Q" at the top of this page. See if you can concentrate on it for 30 seconds without taking your eyes away or losing your attention. Some people can do this right away but most of us have to practice. Whenever you want to practice, pick a small object in your environment and keep focused on it without moving. Time yourself and gradually increase your time.

Q: **Where are all the shells? I love shells and I expected to see a lot under the water while snorkeling but I don't see *any*. Where did they go?**

A: Cheer up! Bivalves and gastropods are all around you. However, they don't look the same as they do in the shell shop so you must get accustomed to seeing them underwater. On the reef, clams, cowries, conches and their relatives are camouflaged by encrusted algae, bits of sponge, bryozoans and so forth. I see shellfish colored black, pink, red and other colors that blend in perfectly with the backgrounds. Also, many are found inside holes, hanging upside down from ledges and in other cryptic environments. In fresh water, the shellfish may be brown or grey to match the underlying mud of the bottom.

If I'm looking for shells, I usually search by shape. When I find bumps on rocks that are shaped like snails, they are usually snails. I also look for an opening and closing slit or water movement. When I see these, there's usually a clam or similar bivalve around.

Q: **What are some of your favorite strokes, floats and snorkeling positions?**

A: I like to turn with a circular movement of one fin tip. I often turn around by pulling in my knees, rolling one-quarter turn in the water, and then straightening out again. I like to do the *skater stroke* with my hands clasped behind my back and my thumb clenched in the fingers of the other hand. I also like to do the *coffin float*, with ankles crossed and both hands crossed against my chest. Both these positions make sure you won't scare creatures away by flailing your arms. For more strokes, see Chapter 4.

Q: **Wes, I kick my fins but I do not go forward. I seem to have to spend a lot more effort than other snorkelers around me and I get tired real early in the day. Suggestions?**

A: This is much more common than you would expect. Check with other snorkelers in the evening after a day of snorkeling and some of them will be beat for the same reason. There are a number of potential solutions to this problem:

- ☑ Changing your stroke can sometimes provide propulsion that is more efficient. Envision your leg as a single unit extending from your hip to the end of your flipper tip. Kick from your hip with the entire length of your legs. Keep your knees stiff but not locked. If done correctly this will result in a rocking, rolling motion. If you have ever seen the way a bulldog's butt moves when he is walking along the sidewalk, that is the motion you want while kicking.

- ☑ Be aware that stiff fins require much more effort to kick than flexible fins. On one trip, I had a pair of thick, rigid fins that required too much effort in the water. I kicked and kicked as hard as I could but I could not go anywhere. I was forced to buy a more flexible pair on the island, which worked perfectly. If your fins are too stiff, trade with someone else and see what a more flexible pair feels like. If you are handy, you can fine-tune your fins to the optimum flexibility for you. See Chapter 3.

- ☑ Remember to use your arms to augment your legs for more propulsion. Check Chapter 4 for arm paddling methods and remember to cup your hands. You can also try using a shallow *frog kick* instead of a *scissors kick*. Sometimes I will snorkel all day long without ever kicking my legs up and down in the water.

- ☑ Check that you have not been swimming into a current. I periodically get the sense that I am swimming like crazy without getting anywhere, when I notice that a current has been pushing me backward all the while. Try moving closer to the shore where currents may be weaker.

- ☑ Propulsion problems seem to be more common on the first day of a snorkeling trip, so do not lose hope. Get a good night's sleep and try tomorrow. By the way, you may also want to find a group of snorkelers who travel more leisurely. There, the problem's solved.

Q: What is the most important piece of snorkeling gear?

A: Your mask. Everything else can be dispensed with if necessary.

Q: Wes, I borrowed a mask from my cousin without trying it. Now that I'm on the island, I found out it leaks. What can I do?

A: All the books tell you to check around the seal between the mask and the lenses for hidden pinpoint holes. Go back to your residence, turn the mask face down and fill it with 1 inch of water. Check it in an hour to see if any water has collected around the lens or anywhere else outside the mask. I had such a leak a long time ago with an old mask. If you have such a leak, you can try some traditional remedies, like rubbing beeswax around the junction between the lens and the mask or simply buy silicone sealant at an automobile store and recaulk the joint.

Usually, you will not be able to find anything wrong with your mask. Then you will either have to empty your mask a lot or buy a new one.

Q: My mask fits fine and does not leak but water still gets in. I can't afford to buy another. What can I do?

A: If you cannot find a leak around the lens, run your fingers around the outside skirt and make sure there is no hair between your face and the mask seal. If you have facial hair, trim it.

Or, try running your fingers over the seal of the mask where it touches your face to see if you can feel tiny cracks. Sometimes there is a ridge of plastic flashing left over from the molding process breaking the seal between the mask skirt and your face. Often you can carefully trim away such ridges with a utility knife or straight-jawed nail clippers.

Q: I do not know what is wrong with my mask. Unless I really tighten it hard, it leaks. I end up looking like somebody has been sucking my face with a toilet plunger and sometimes it still leaks. My boyfriend tried to adjust it but he just screwed it up worse than it was. Help!

A: There is a limit to how far you can tighten your mask strap without imploding your face. My face is difficult to fit and I have spent many evenings being teased about mask-face. Try scrunching your face up like a prune as you put on your mask. After the mask is in place, relax your face muscles and it may fit tighter.

Ultimately, you will have to stop squashing your kisser. Beg, borrow or buy a mask that fits well and your life will be good again. If your face is small, try on smaller youth masks. See Chapter 2.

Q: I went out snorkeling this morning and I think there's something wrong with my eyes. Usually I see great, but all of a sudden, everything was blurry. Do you have any thoughts on this?

A: Unexpected fuzzy vision can be daunting. Let's review a few potential causes:

- ☑ **Mask Fogging**. Check to make sure the lenses in your mask are fog free. Take off your mask in the water and rinse the inside surface of the lens. Then quickly put your mask back on and check to see if your vision is now clear. If fogging is the problem, it will soon build up again, so check Chapter 2 for defogging strategies before you go out again next time.
- ☑ **Smudges**. Greasy fingerprints on the outside of the lens can also cause blurry vision. With the mask on, rub the outside of the lens with the back of your thumb. Unless you eat chicharrones for breakfast, most smudges come from wayward sunscreen and/or insect repellant. The back of the thumb is the spot most often missed by the goo, so try a quick wipe.
- ☑ **Dry Eyes**. When some people put on their masks, they pull up on their forehead skin so hard that it becomes difficult to blink. You can tell this in a partner if they wear a perpetually surprised expression. Unless you blink periodically, your eyes will dry out, so loosen up your mask and try some eye drops.
- ☑ **Poor Visibility**. Once I went out for a second snorkel after lunch and I couldn't see anything. Strong currents were stirring up the bottom and the amazing Caribbean water clarity was gone. Wait and try again later.
- ☑ **Eye Strain**. A long day of looking can strain the eyes and cause blurriness, especially if you are accustomed to wearing glasses. The problem worsens when the light decreases, because when your pupils dilate, your tired eye muscles have to work harder to focus. Once while hurrying to finish an environmental impact report, I spent too many hours staring into my microscope without resting my eyes. Over the course of several days, my eyes began to blur until my vision went black and I was completely blind for a few hours. That gave me some time to ponder good ocular hygiene until my vision returned.
- ☑ **Bad Stuff**. If a friend and/or diving partner comes to you with sudden loss of vision in one eye, blind spots or a sense that a curtain was pulled across one eye, and has been at high altitude or is at risk for glaucoma, stroke or heart disease, get them to an emergency room PDQ. Sometimes these vision changes can be a sign of other, internal problems.

Q: **I hate my rubber mask strap. It pulls my hair and hurts my scalp all the time I'm snorkeling and I have to comb out snarls when I get home. Any clever tricks up your sleeve for this?**

A: I never use silicone straps on my masks any more. As soon as I get a new mask, I tear off the silicone strap forthwith and replace it with a neoprene strap that does not attack my hair or ears. These straps are somewhat stretchy and they can be adjusted to hold the mask firmly without putting excess pressure on your face. They slide through the mask buckles and provide infinite adjustment, usually with Velcro connectors. See Chapter 3.

Q: **What do I do about the seawater? It tastes so bad and I always end up swallowing a mouthful.**

A: If you cannot tolerate the bitter, salty seawater in your mouth, spit it out. The trick is to suck all the moisture from your mouth and spit it into your snorkel. It will empty from your snorkel and your mouth will produce more saliva to replace the nasty ocean water. Afterwards, try to determine what happened *before* you were surprised with a spurt of seawater in your mouth. Did you dip the tip of your snorkel under water? If so, block off the mouthpiece with your tongue before you dive below the surface. Did you get a mouthful because your snorkel leaks or because the mouthpiece doesn't fit your mouth? Get it attended to.

Q: **I've seen some fins with notches or hinges half way down the flipper part. Do you recommend these?**

A: The manufacturer's advertisements say "buenos notches," but I say keep notches off your flippers for reasons of simple mechanics. If we plotted the flexibility of your flipper from the tip to the base on a graph, you would see a smooth curve with greatest flexibility at the tip and greatest stiffness near your toes. When you bend your flipper in the water, the energy is released in proportion to the degree that the fin is flexed when you kick. With experience, you learn how much to flex your fins to get exactly the right thrust to power you through the water, make tight banking turns around fire coral, slide through water channels in the rocks or precisely counter the power of a wave so you can stay in one spot against the current. Notches, hinges, or other devices mess up fins' smooth flexion and make it harder to maneuver in the water. Eschew these tricky fins.

Q: **I bought fancy fins that have grooves and ridges across the surface of the fin that are supposed to smooth the passage of water in diving. I thought this must be good until I read your book and I became worried. Will these gimmicky fins be OK for snorkeling?**

A: Fear not. I have used fins with every manner of groove and ridge and I have never found that they made the slightest bit of difference, good or bad. They will be fine.

Someday when you have extra time, you could consider paring off the surplus ridges, or just wait until you need new fins and get a simpler design.

Q: **Do you know of anything to put in your ear to stop earache?**

A: Traditionally one of two solutions has been put in the ear. The oldest is olive oil, which you may be able to find in a pharmacy under the name of "sweet oil." The other is a mixture of white vinegar and ethyl alcohol like Everclear. However, I am suspicious of these nostrums. If you have an ear infection or injury, I strongly advise you to see your doctor before putting home remedies in your ears.

Q: **What is "dead foot disease?"**

A: "Dead foot disease" and "stinky boot syndrome" are common names for fungal infections that develop on feet, footwear and neoprene wetsuits when they are damp. These can be hard to control. In the past, I have had to throw away footwear contaminated by this stinky infestation to keep it from spreading to my other gear. I once had a large, expensive suitcase ruined after catching this smelly infection from damp booties. On your feet, dead foot disease is a real turnoff. Imagine sitting down to breakfast when you smell something resembling carrion. You look around and finally discover that the offending objects are your own tootsies. By that time, everyone else has discovered the same thing and they move away in fear and disgust, holding their noses and cursing beneath their breath. It's not a pretty sight.

Treating this problem is a challenge because you can stimulate fungal growth by applying anything containing water. Initially I bought myriad solutions sold to rehabilitate smelly wetsuits, but I found that most of these were just perfumes that smelled worse than the dead feet. Currently, I spritz Listerine, Bactine or rubbing alcohol in my booties and shoes. I rub these solutions over my feet and toes and let them dry in the sun. This regimen is working well so far.

Q: **What do you do if you suddenly find yourself carried off course by the ocean? This happened to me last summer. I had to swim as hard as I could just to stay in place and I became pretty exhausted.**

A: Strong currents or even strong winds can push you way off course or even out to sea. If you find yourself bucking a current or headwind or the waves get too choppy to swim in, don't hesitate to swim to shore or the nearest boat and leave the water. If you have to walk back to your entry point or cut your snorkeling outing short, it is a small price to pay to ensure your own safety. There's no place for heroics in snorkeling. See Chapter 9.

Q: **I'm so clumsy that I'm always bumping into coral with my body or fins. I'm hurting myself, ruining my gear, and I'm sure I'm destroying these microhabitats. How can I stop messing things up?**

A: Clumsiness comes from inattentiveness and a poor sense of your body position. Teach yourself by going out with no fins, no dive skin and the smallest swimsuit you can find. This will help you become more aware of the location of your body in space. I do this exercise periodically to help maintain my own self-awareness in the water. Be aware that painful stings can result from brushing fire coral, spiny urchins and their colleagues. If you are on the watch for these, you will be practicing and improving your attention.

Q: I don't know why you think everyone should be so paranoid about safety. I went alone on a snorkeling trip last year and didn't take any precautions and I'm fine.

A: I hope your luck holds out.

Q: Do you snorkel at night?

A: I went snorkeling at night once. At night, the diving lamp was as bright as a laser. I could barely look at it. When I turned my light on an eel in his hole, he was so frightened that I was ashamed and I never went out at night again. If humans cannot be respectful of other creatures, at least we can try to be compassionate.

Q: I saw a man swim out to rescue an iguana who was 30 feet from shore. What do you think about that?

A: I applaud all efforts to learn about and respect nature and the living creatures that comprise it. This person might have saved a life and it was good for his soul. However, I have noticed iguanas swimming quite well on their own and it is possible that this person was just playing chauffer to a lizard who had everything under control.

Unfortunately, it is hard to know what is helpful and what is harmful when you interfere with animals and their environment. You just have to let prudence be your guide and most of all, be sure that you do no harm, even if it is unintentional.

Q: I have a nice pair of salt-water fish in my aquarium. Do you think it would be a good idea to take them along and give them a new home in the Caribbean?

A: For heaven's sake, don't introduce non-native species to a new environment. Some of the worst pests in the world were originally non-native species introduced to new environments where they messed up the new ecosystem and crowded out indigenous species. Horrible, bottom-feeding carp with scales like guitar picks were introduced into the Mississippi River with disastrous results. The pigeons who now foul and disfigure our cities and spread histoplasmosis and cryptococcosis were originally introduced as a food delicacy.

Q: What do you think about eating highly seasoned foods before snorkeling?

A: Hot, spicy foods can exacerbate stomach irritation and they can mimic a heart attack. Also, I enjoy spicy foods greatly and I eat them whenever possible.

Q: What do you eat on the days when you are snorkeling?

A: I eat fruit, vegetables and protein from fish, meat, eggs and cheese. My favorite snorkeling fruits are guava, mango, papaya and fresh pineapple. I drink water, soda or sometimes beer during the day. I eschew starches like bagels, biscuits, bread, Danish, muffins, potatoes, scones and breakfast cereal including oatmeal and granola. I sometimes eat muesli. I wait a while after eating before I go into the water but I doubt that it is really necessary.

Q: What do you think about drinking? Should I go out on the town all night with the others in my resort?

A: You'll see many older and especially larger individuals who stay up all night drinking and smoking and then dive like crazy the next day. Staying up all night and getting loaded is fine when you're young—I guess—but if you are more mature in years and/or wisdom then you should use some common sense and restraint.

Personally, I like the world. I like what's in it. My experience of reality does not improve with the addition of distilled bonhomie, Dutch courage, spirited inhibition or toxic sedation, especially when I'll be in the ocean all the next day. Tired people make mistakes and a mistake in the ocean can mean anything from a nasty fire coral gash to being carried off by an unexpected current and mashed against the rocks. Be safe and preserve enough brain cells to enjoy your snorkeling.

Q: What's your usual schedule on a snorkeling day?

A: I rise at 6:00 am, breakfast from 6:30 to 7:00 am, nap from 7:00 to 7:30 am, snorkel from 8:00 to 11:00 am, read or nap from 11:30 am to 12:00 pm, and I lunch from 12:00 to 12:30 pm. Then I snorkel from 1:00 to 4:00 pm and I relax from 4:30 to 5:00 pm. I sometimes have a drink at 5:30 pm, and I eat dinner at 6:00 pm.

Q: I spent my holiday at a resort inn at Jamaica last year where they have a huge shallow area a few steps from the pool and bar to snorkel. The trouble is, I never saw anything but sand.

A: The snorkeling area to which you refer has a counterpart in many resorts. It is created by bulldozing an area near the shore to flatten the bottom and remove all life from the water. Sometimes fine sand is imported, carted in and dumped on the natural bottom. On one occasion, I worked my hand down through the sand in such a swimming area and found a concrete slab. Periodically, the staff members go through the entire roped-off area and pull up or chase off any signs of life in order to ensure the pristine white and sterile substrate. If you want to snorkel the reef, you must do it somewhere else than these synthetic swimming abominations.

Q: What do I do about the sand? It's on my floor, in all my shoes and even in the bed. I wake in the middle of the night chewing on it and scouring my teeth to the dentin. It rubs my feet raw like sandpaper. Help!

A: Sorry, Charlie. It's a fact that when you live near the ocean, sand will find its way into your home and possessions. I do have a few tricks for you to try, however:

- ☑ Whenever you exit the water, develop a habit of shaking your feet off in the ocean. If there are many waves, you may still end up with some sand sticking to your feet and ankles but it will decrease the amount of sand that you carry from the ocean into your home.
- ☑ After you leave the water, let your legs dry off before trying to remove the sand. Dry sand can be removed much easier than wet sand.
- ☑ Use a soft brush to coax sand off your feet and body instead of wiping it off with a towel. The towel just moves the sand around and drops it back on your body or on the floor.
- ☑ Set aside one or two pairs of footwear that will never be worn near the sand. Try to keep these clean and you'll have something to wear that will not scrub the skin from your feet.

Q: You said to avoid currents, but everywhere I go I run into currents. They bounce me around so much I'm afraid of banging into the reef.

A: This is not good. You cannot snorkel in 3 feet of water if the waves are throwing you around. Here are my suggestions:

- ☑ Try different times of the day, including early morning and late afternoon.
- ☑ Find a snorkeling site more protected from the wind.
- ☑ Move into slightly deeper water.

By adjusting for these variables, you should be able to find quieter water. In the future, make sure you are coming in the season where the ocean is the quietest or choose a different destination. Use the Internet to find out more details.

Q: What kind of sunglasses should I bring on my snorkeling trip?

A: Do not bring $300 designer sunglasses on your snorkeling trip. Sunglasses get lost. Salt in the sea breeze eats off lens coatings and blowing sand invariably causes a pattern of fine scratches across the lenses. I buy industrial safety glasses a dozen at a time from an industrial supply company. They are made of impact-resistant, UV-blocking polycarbonate tinted neutral grey. They are manufactured to close government tolerances and are remarkably inexpensive. I found out about them by observing which sunglasses professional baseball players wear. See the Appendix for sources.

Q: **I have a fixed budget to spend on snorkeling clothing and equipment. How should I divide the money up?**

A: I suggest that you splurge on the following:

- ☑ **Sunscreen**. Do not leave yourself vulnerable to cancer. Buy the best sunscreen available. Check with your doctor, dermatologist or local pharmacist if you are not sure which brand is best.

- ☑ **Mask**. You cannot see anything without a mask. A good mask is vital for a satisfactory snorkeling experience. Moreover, you will have to live with leakage and any other quirks every minute you are snorkeling. Even when I was a student, wearing jeans and breathing through a sawed off piece of tubing, I saved my pennies to get a great, low-volume mask. You do not have to have the most expensive mask, just one that is good for you. Find the best-fitting low-volume mask with the widest field of view that you can afford. Before you buy a mask, make sure that you understand the seller's return policy. You may have to shop around until you find exactly what you want. See Chapter 2.

On the other hand, you can scrimp and save on your:

- ☑ **Snorkel**. Any snorkel will do. A purge valve near the mouth is desirable, but if you find an old snorkel in an attic or garage sale, it will probably be OK. If it is curved at the top or has a ping pong ball in a cage, just cut the top tubing off straight and you will be fine. If water gets into your open snorkel, just blow it out with a lungful of air.

- ☑ **Pull-on Fins**: If you want to save a little money, buy some inexpensive pull-on fins. These are often available from yard sales, attics and neighbors' garages, and they will work satisfactorily until you want something better. Make sure that you try them on before you walk away with them to make sure they fit. Pull-on fins should fit closely enough that they stay on if you flail your legs around but they must be comfortable. They must be long enough that your toes do not get pinched in the front of the foot pockets. You may have to wet your feet to get them in the fins, but if your feet ache after wearing the fins for a few minutes, they are too tight. If there is a hole for your toes, make sure the surround does not bind or chafe. If there is a seam or some plastic flashing inside that rubs on your foot, leave the fins behind or be prepared to perform surgery to smooth the foot pocket. If there is a tear around the mouth of the foot pocket on either fin, forget about them.

If you are still too undecided about snorkeling to make a monetary investment in your own equipment, borrow or rent a mask, snorkel and fins from the diving store or front desk at your resort. These will most likely be a sunny yellow color, really flexible and look like they were designed for kids—which they probably were. If you are concerned about cleanliness and disease, wash the snorkel mouthpiece with Listerine and dry it before using. Alternatively, you can pony up and buy the cheapest snorkel you can find and it will probably be fine.

Q: **Yesterday my wife and I met some divers who said, "You snorkelers must be crazy. We can't believe you come all the way here and all you do is snorkel. We SCUBA dive and yesterday we saw two nurse sharks and a lemon shark and an octopus and a seahorse in just one 20-minute dive." We felt embarrassed for snorkeling. What do I say to these guys?**

A: You could say, "Yesterday I snorkeled near the reef for 10 minutes and I saw a banded butterfly fish, a beaugregory, a bicolor damselfish, a blue angelfish, some blue tang, a bluehead wrasse, a bridled goby, a bristled fireworm, several Christmas tree worms, a clown wrasse, a cocoa damselfish, some crabs, a dusky damselfish, a few fairy basslets, fanworms, a French angelfish, a grey angelfish, a needlefish, an octopus, a peacock flounder, a princess parrotfish, a queen parrotfish, a rainbow parrotfish, some red-lipped blennies, a slender filefish, a smooth trunkfish, a spotted moray eel, a stoplight parrotfish, a striped grunt, a trumpet fish, some yellow goatfish, a yellowhead wrasse and a yellowtail damselfish." At least that's what *I* saw when I was snorkeling this morning.

However, it is politer just to smile and say, "Good for you! Isn't the ocean a wonderful place?" and leave it at that.

Q: **You have warned about storms, currents and waves on the ocean. Are the waves on the Great Lakes also dangerous?**

A: Waves on large lakes can be more dangerous than ocean waves because they are less predictable. Wind and storms can stir up huge waves on large lakes. However, unlike ocean tides, strong winds blowing across the Great Lakes can change the water levels by several feet in a short time. Furthermore, large, treacherous lake waves can break in many directions at once, unpredictably. This is why the floors of the Great Lakes are littered with sunken craft. Always be careful of wind and storms when snorkeling on large lakes. If you are in doubt, get out.

Q: **I have a burning question I am embarrassed to ask. What do I do if I am in the ocean and I need to pee?**

A: Not surprisingly, this is a question many people want to ask. Because of increased pressure on your body, swimming has a diuretic effect. Children gleefully use the ocean as their bathroom, but I recommend that you void at home before you go out on any snorkeling excursion and again just before you go in the water, if you feel the need. If you are caught away from facilities, find some bushes or other cover. If you are too modest to do this, then you will have to hold it or go back to the closest public restroom.

APPENDIX
RESOURCES AND BIBLIOGRAPHY

There are almost an unlimited number of resources available today if you know where to look. The following references will help you get started. You will find Internet sites that can provide you with masks, fins, and snorkels as well as the specialty items mentioned in *The Ultimate Snorkeling Book*. To follow up on the ecological ideas discussed above, there are links that will help you participate in cleaning up and protecting our natural habitats, supporting endangered aquatic creatures, and helping to make and change political policies. You will also find a book list containing snorkeling and natural history books to help enrich your snorkeling experience, philosophy books to help you grow mentally and spiritually, travel guides to help you plan your trips, and even some health books to combat anxiety and depression you might encounter.

SOURCES FOR SNORKELING GEAR

You can find a lot of good gear over the Internet. Note that the back-order and return policies of on-line venders are quite variable, so check before you buy. If you are in doubt, the Better Business Bureau keeps a list of shady venders. The general rule is, "If it seems to be too good or too cheap to be true, it probably is."

A. G. Russell Knives. I say, leave the knives at home for safety's sake. However, if you have to take one, get a good blade that will cut food and not fingers. I use a knife made of VG10 steel for cooking. http://www.agrussell.com

Amazon.com. "We've got snorkeling gear." With over 350 different mask models, I couldn't get myself to count the brands. http://www.amazon.com

Betadine. Find out everything you want to know about that most wonderful of germicidal soaps manufactured by Purdue Pharma. Betadine is the povidone iodine liquid soap used by surgeons worldwide to kill germs before operating. I buy it in bulk. http://www.betadine.com

Dive Goddess. The best and wildest nylon dive skins for snorkelers. I have used many of their products and I love these gals. http://www.divegoddess.com

Divers Supply. A large online store for SCUBA divers that carries many brands of gear that snorkelers will covet. http://www.divers-supply.com

Dolphin SCUBA Center. With a website and stores located in Sacramento and Stockton, California, Dolphin provides convenient shopping for snorkelers around the world. http://www.dolphinscuba.com

Joe Diver America. Hey Joe! He has plenty of SCUBA-oriented gear that snorkelers will love. This is also a great site for children's gear. http://www.joediveramerica.com

Laboratory Safety Supply. In their latest catalog, I counted 66 different styles of safety glasses you can use as sunglasses. There is some cool stuff here that you won't see at your optician's or sunglasses store. Plus, LSS lenses are shatterproof, color-corrected grey, and block ultraviolet rays. So go here and buy sunglasses. Single orders are OK, but I usually buy plenty over the course of a year. While you're there, check the first aid kits (35 styles), eyeglass cords (7 styles in 14 colors), earplugs (32 styles), gloves (50 styles), floating sunglass cases, and eyeglass cleaners. Go for it! You can order by telephone at 800-356-0783 or online. http://www.lss.com

Pelican Bags. The Pelican Company makes my luggage and equipment cases. They're a little heavier than some, but they are waterproof, they float, they come in all sizes and they are guaranteed against breakage. Pelican even makes little waterproof boxes in which you can store your toiletries so they don't leak all over the inside of your bag. Visit their website and become a Pelican convert. They make cool flashlights, too. http://www.pelican-case.com

SCUBA.com. They list a whopping 45 brands of masks and also have some good equipment information. http://www.scuba.com

Sea Vision. I use Sea Vision masks. Go to their online site and choose the size, color, lens tint and prescription to custom build your own mask. This company sold me on their color correction. No matter what mask you wear, you have to come here to order Sea Vision Defog. It is simply the best. http://www.seavisionusa.com

Snorkel Bob's. "We build our own gear." That means they carry fewer brands, but you'll still find a lot of snorkeling gear from which to choose. http://snorkelbob.com

Snorkel City. "The snorkeling superstore." The last time I visited, they had only two brands of masks, and one of them was the Snorkel City brand. However, they have a prescription mask service. http://www.snorkelcity.com

Tilley Hats. If you do something, do it right. That's what Alex Tilley has done with hats. Go to his website and get the best darn sun hat you've ever had. Do it now! http://www.tilley.com

CONSERVATION GROUPS

Mother Nature will not survive without our help. Now that you know more about the aquatic environment, find out how you can help preserve it. These groups can help.

American Cetacean Society. The oldest whale conservation group in the world is nonprofit and dedicated to protecting "whales, dolphins, porpoises and their habitats through public education, research grants, and conservation actions." http://www.acsonline.org

Greenpeace. A sometimes aggressive, often political, "independent global campaigning organization that acts to change attitudes and behavior, to protect and conserve the environment, and to promote peace." They have a wide variety of programs including marine conservation efforts. It's really a way of life. http://www.greenpeace.org

IEMANYA Oceanica. This organization is dedicated to the worldwide conservation of sharks, rays, and their habitats. In case you wondered, IEMANYA stands for Investigacion, Educacion, Manejo y Asesoria (Research, Education, Management and Advice). http://www.iemanya.org

Marine Conservation Biology Institute. A nonprofit organization with a mission to "advance the science of marine conservation biology and secure protection for ocean ecosystems." http://www.mcbi.org

National Audubon Society. Known for their work with birds, this hoary environmental organization is dedicated to conservation and has some international and marine projects including the protection of whales. http://www.audubon.org

The Nature Conservancy. Their mission is "to preserve the plants, animals and natural communities that represent the diversity of life on Earth by protecting the lands and waters they need to survive." They sponsor a variety of marine conservation programs. http://www.nature.org

Ocean Conservancy. This not-for-profit organization sponsors coastal cleanup projects and targets government legislation. http://www.oceanconservancy.org

Oceanic Society. This nonprofit conservation organization's mission is "to protect endangered wildlife and preserve threatened marine habitats worldwide." They emphasize the establishment of nature preserves, support scientific research and promote eco-education. http://www.oceanicsociety.org

REEF. The Reef Environmental Education Foundation is a tax-exempt, charitable organization that works with Florida National Marine Sanctuary and the Natural Parks Service. It is "a grass-roots organization that seeks to conserve marine ecosystems by educating, enlisting and enabling divers and other marine enthusiasts to become active ocean stewards and citizen scientists." http://www.reef.org

The Sea Turtle Restoration Project. Under the parent organization of Turtle Island Restoration Network, The Sea Turtle Restoration Project "fights to protect endangered sea turtles in ways that make cultural and economic sense to the communities that share the beaches and waters with these gentle creatures." There is no better time to start than now. Their telephone is 415-663-8590, and you may email them at info@seaturtles.org. http://www.seaturtles.org

World Wildlife Foundation. Like the name says, a one-stop shop for global conservation efforts. They can help you get hands-on experience helping endangered species. I argued with an executive to hold a joint fundraiser with the World Wrestling Foundation (WWF), but they were not amused. http://www.worldwildlife.org

SNORKELING REFERENCE BOOKS

Here are some references that you may find useful in the pursuit of your snorkeling sport.

Richard Dawkins. *The Selfish Gene*. Oxford University Press, 2006.
   An introduction to population biology and a discussion of an interesting spider species I reported.

Ned DeLoach with Paul Humann. *Reef Fish Behavior* New World Publications, 1999.
Paul Humann, edited by Ned DeLoach. *Reef Fish Identification*. New World Publications, 1999.
Paul Humann and Ned DeLoach. *Snorkeling Guide to Marine Life*. New World Publications, 1995, 80 pages.
Paul Humann and Ned DeLoach. Reef *Creature Identification*. New World Publications, 1992.
   These Paul Humann and Ned DeLoach volumes are my favorite reef books. I read them on the plane to and from the islands, and almost every day on my trip to find out what I am seeing on my snorkeling excursions. The books contain information on species identification and absolutely beautiful illustrations. If you want to identify fish and invertebrate creatures on the reef, you should buy these books.

Bob French. *Snorkeling...Here's How*. Lonely Planet Publications, 1995, 32 pages. This venerable book was one of the first to discuss how to evaluate and purchase snorkeling equipment.

John Newman. *Scuba Diving and Snorkeling for Dummies*. For Dummies Publications, 1999. I like this book. Written in the familiar dummies format, it is a fun read. However, as the title suggests, the book is heavily slanted toward SCUBA divers.

Wes Burgess and Evelyn Shaw. Development and ecology of fish schooling. In Paul R. Ryan, Editor, *Harvesting the Sea*. Van Nostrand Press, New York, 1985.

You may also wish to consult my naturalist publications in such journals as *Scientific American, Ecology, Ethology and Sociobiology, Animal Behavior, Behavioral and Neural Biology, The American Midland Naturalist, Psyche, Symposia of the Zoological Society of London*, and others.

SNORKELING PHILOSOPHY

If you have found my philosophical comments about snorkeling interesting, you may wish to read further.

Wes Burgess. The Tao Te Ching by Lao Tse. Traditional Taoist Wisdom to Enlighten Everyone. Volume 1 of the Clear Mind Series. CreateSpace, 2012.
Wes Burgess. The Tao Te Ching by Lao Tse. Mini Edition. CreateSpace, 2012.
Wes Burgess. The Gateless Gate of Zen. Traditional Wisdom, Koans and Stories to Enlighten Everyone. Volume 2 of The Clear Mind Series. CreateSpace, 2012.
Wes Burgess. The Gateless Gate of Zen. Mini Edition. CreateSpace, 2012.
Wes Burgess. Calm Your Mind: Exercises to Reduce Stress, Improve Focus, and Control Anxiety, Anger, and Depression. CreateSpace, 2011.
Wes Burgess. Be Enlightened! A Guidebook to the Tao Te Ching and Taoist Meditation. CreateSpace, 2010.
   The clear mind exhorted by these ancient authors reminds me of floating in the warm ocean.

Thomas Cleary and J. C. Cleary, translators. Hsyeg Tou. *The Blue Cliff Record.* Shambhala Press, 1992. An ancient and exciting book of Zen puzzles to broaden your awareness.

J. P. Das, John R. Kirby, Ronald F. Jarman. *Simultaneous and Successive Cognitive Processes.* Academic Press, 1979. Learn more about how your brain works in this book. It seems to me that humans occupy themselves with successive cognitive tasks whereas fish seem to use more simultaneous brain processing. See what you think.

Julian Jaynes. *The Origin of Consciousness in the Breakdown of the Bicameral Mind.* Houghton Mifflin Company, 1976. An interesting story about how our modern mind might have evolved, with some useful neurological information thrown in.

J. Krishnamurti. (D. Rajagopal, editor.) *Commentaries on Living.* 1st, 2nd and 3rd *Series.* Penguin Books, 2006.

J. Krishnamurti. (D. Rajagopal, editor.) *Think on these Things.* Harper Perennial, 1989.
Krishnamurti was hailed as the next Messiah but he renounced that honor to teach a philosophy of objectivity.

D. C. Lau, translator. Lao Tzu. *Tao Te Ching.* Penguin Press, 1963. One of my favorite translations of the book of philosophical precepts by the ancient Chinese scholar.

Red Pine, translator. *The Zen Teaching of Bodhidharma,* North Point Press, 1989. A rare look at the teachings of the Indian monk who founded what is now known as Zen.

Paul Reps, editor. *Zen Flesh, Zen Bones.* Penguin Books, 2000. This is a very accessible collection of stories and puzzles that are used by Zen teachers to broaden their students' awareness.

W. H. D. Rouse, editor. *Great Dialogues of Plato.* Signet, 1999. This is a readable compendium of the writings of that most Eastern of Western philosophers, Plato.

Irmgard Schloegl. *The Zen Teaching of Rinzai.* Shambhala Press, 1975. Rinzai renounced the reverence of scripture and encouraged his students to find out about life on their own.

Ludwig Wittgenstein, *Tractatus Logico-Philosophicus*, Routledge and Kegan Paul, 1977.

Ludwig Wittgenstein. *Zettel.* Edited by G. E. M. Anscombe and G. H. Von Wright. Univ. of California Press, 1970.

Ludwig Wittgenstein. *The Blue and Brown Books.* Harper, 1958.
Wittgenstein was one of the most influential philosophers of the last century, helping to clarify the difference between language and real experiences.

TRAVEL GUIDES

Lonely Planet and Pieces publish guidebooks with lots of useful, extra material. The books typically begin with a brief review of local diving sites including some with snorkeling potential, how to get there, what time of day is best, etc. The books are also stuffed with reviews of topside attractions such as accommodations, hot nightspots and interesting vacation activities. If you need a good guidebook, I recommend all of them highly.

ANXIETY AND MOOD PROBLEMS

Wes Burgess. *Calm Your Mind: Exercises to Reduce Stress, Improve Focus, and Control Anxiety, Anger, and Depression.* CreateSpace, 2011.

Wes Burgess. *The Mental Status Examination.* CreateSpace, 2011.

Wes Burgess. *Transtorno Bipolar. Perguntas da Vida Real com Prespostas Atualizadas.* Editora Gaia, São Paulo, Brazil, 2010. (Portuguese)

Wes Burgess. *The Depression Answer Book.* Sourcebooks, 2009.

Wes Burgess. *The Bipolar Handbook for Children, Teens, and Families.* Avery/Penguin Press, 2008.

Wes Burgess. *Guia del Bipolar.* Ediciones Robinbook, Barcelona, Spain, 2007. (Spanish)

Wes Burgess. *The Bipolar Handbook.* Avery/Penguin Press, 2006.

If you have concerns about your emotions before or during a trip or if you wonder whether you have a clinical disorder, I invite you to consult my clinical books. They contain information on relaxation exercises, meditation, nutrition and how to treat mental and emotional problems.

DISCLAIMER

The information in this book is one author's point of view. In all cases, follow your own best judgment and keep safe in every situation. Always follow your doctors' and specialists' advice on your own physical limitations. Never take chances with your life or those of your loved ones. Always remember to have fun and keep snorkeling fun for everyone!

THE AUTHOR

Wes Burgess, M.D., Ph.D., is a lifetime snorkeler and the author of books, book chapters, columns and articles about animal and human behavior, behavioral biology, ecology, fish behavior and development, medicine and psychology in publications like *Scientific American, Oceanus, Ecology,* and *Animal Behavior*. He holds doctorate degrees in Zoology and Medicine and he has taught at Stanford University, UCLA, University of California at Davis, and other major institutions. He has given lectures, workshops and symposia around the world.

Wes lives within walking distance of the ocean with his wife and two dogs. When he is not writing or snorkeling, you can find him flying two-line stunt kites on the beach.

EPILOG:
THE SONG OF THE FIREWORM

Sometime in the far future, a bearded fireworm
Will poke his fiery head out of the waves as if to say,

"Years, what are years?"

And, there being no one to reply,
He will pull his head beneath the waves again
And go about his business, the same way his kind have done
Since the beginning of the world.

And the ocean foam will whisper,
"Man, woman, where are you?"

But there will be no reply
And the ocean will go on without us, the same as it has done
Since the beginning of the world.

So I say to those who share the waves today,
Let's emulate the wise old fireworm
And try to stick around as long as we can.

Printed in Poland
by Amazon Fulfillment
Poland Sp. z o.o., Wrocław